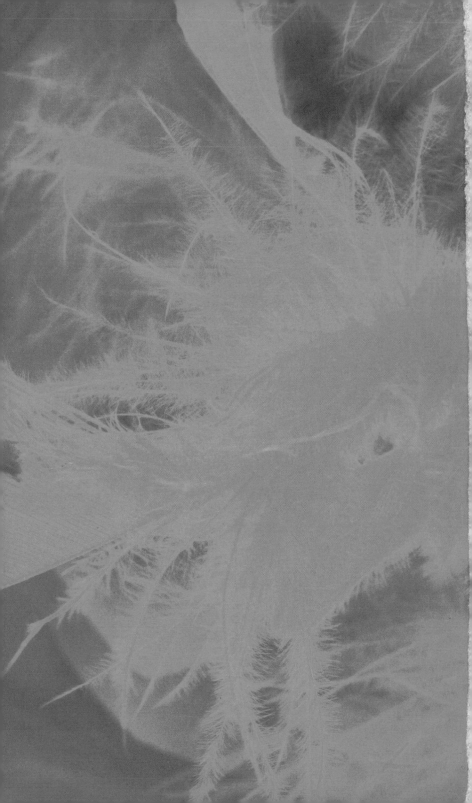

Praise for *What Is Your Self-Worth?*

"Cheryl Saban shows us that we each possess the power to free ourselves from the restraints others would place upon us. Her book makes it clear that we define our worth in this world and we each have a special strength and determination to shape our lives. This work is a triumphant declaration of women's independence."
— **Nancy Pelosi,** Speaker of the House of Representatives

"Dr. Cheryl Saban has dedicated her expertise, compassion, and resources to improving the lives of others, especially children and women. As an author, psychologist, activist, philanthropist, wife, mother, grandmother, and friend, Cheryl has served as a powerful example of how to balance love of family, responsibility to community, and an unyielding commitment to learning and teaching."
— **Barbara Boxer,** U.S. senator

"This book is an important and timely read for everyone—not just women. Cheryl has done an excellent job of bringing attention to a critical issue."
— **Susie Buffett,** chairwoman, The Sherwood Foundation

*"In this masterful book, Cheryl Saban draws upon her tremendous intellect, her vast life experiences, her professional expertise, and her towering humanitarian spirit that propels her extraordinary efforts as a woman/child advocate. **What Is Your Self-Worth?** will surely be an invaluable resource and guide to women as they explore and validate their own self-worth. Both women and men will gain important insights that are integral to our ongoing work as a society to more fully recognize, support, and celebrate the status and contributions of women."*
— **Barbara Firestone, Ph.D.,** president and CEO,
The Help Group

"Every person has more potential and more power than they acknowledge to themselves or exercise in their lives, particularly women. Cheryl Saban helps explain how to unlock that potential by starting with your own sense of self-worth. She will set you on an exciting and rewarding journey. Enjoy the trip."
— **Lady Lynn Forester de Rothschild,** CEO, EL Rothschild

WHAT IS YOUR
SELF-W♥RTH?

Also by Cheryl Saban, Ph.D.

New Mother's Survival Guide

Recipe for Good Parenting: Words of Wisdom <u>for</u> Parents
of All Ages, <u>from</u> Parents of All Ages

Recipe for a Good Marriage: Wise Words and Quirky Advice
for Happy, Long-Lasting Relationships

50 Ways to Save Our Children: Small, Medium, & Big Ways
You Can Change a Child's Life

Sins of the Mother: An Alison Young Thriller

Griffin's Play Group Series

Miracle Child: Genetic Mother, Surrogate Womb

Please visit Hay House USA: **www.hayhouse.com**®
Hay House Australia: **www.hayhouse.com.au**
Hay House UK: **www.hayhouse.co.uk**
Hay House South Africa: **www.hayhouse.co.za**
Hay House India: **www.hayhouse.co.in**

WHAT IS YOUR
SELF-W♥RTH?

A Woman's Guide to Validation

Cheryl Saban, Ph.D.

HAY HOUSE, INC.
Carlsbad, California • New York City
London • Sydney • Johannesburg
Vancouver • Hong Kong • New Delhi

Published and distributed in the United States by: Hay House, Inc.: www.
hayhouse.com • *Published and distributed in Australia by:* Hay House
Australia Pty. Ltd.: www.hayhouse.com.au • *Published and distributed
in the United Kingdom by:* Hay House UK, Ltd.: www.hayhouse.co.uk •
Published and distributed in the Republic of South Africa by: Hay House
SA (Pty), Ltd.: www.hayhouse.co.za • *Distributed in Canada by:* Raincoast:
www.raincoast.com • *Published in India by:* Hay House Publishers India:
www.hayhouse.co.in

Editorial supervision: Jill Kramer • *Design:* Jen Kennedy

The author of this book does not dispense medical advice or prescribe
the use of any technique as a form of treatment for physical, emotional,
or medical problems without the advice of a physician, either directly or
indirectly. The intent of the author is only to offer information of a general
nature to help you in your quest for emotional and spiritual well-being. In
the event you use any of the information in this book for yourself, which
is your constitutional right, the author and the publisher assume no
responsibility for your actions.

Library of Congress Cataloging-in-Publication Data

Saban, Cheryl.
  What is your self-worth? : a woman's guide to validation / Cheryl Saban.
-- 1st ed.
    p. cm.
  ISBN 978-1-4019-2395-2 (hardcover : alk. paper)   1.   Self-esteem in
women. I. Title.
  BF697.5.S46S33 2009
  155.3'33--dc22

                                                            2008042098

ISBN: 978-1-4019-2395-2

12 11 10 09   4 3 2 1
1st edition, May 2009

Printed in the United States of America

To my daughters,
Tifanie, Heidi, and Tanya;
my son, Ness;
my incredible husband, Haim;
my parents, Betty and Ken;
and
my mother-in-law, Virginie,
for knowing and expressing your self-worth
and for always acknowledging mine.

CONTENTS

For attractive lips, speak words of kindness.
For lovely eyes, seek out the good in people.
For a slim figure, share your food with the hungry.
For beautiful hair, let a child run his or her fingers
through it once a day.
For poise, walk with the knowledge you'll never walk alone.
We leave you a tradition with a future.
The tender loving care of human beings
will never become obsolete.
People even more than things have to be restored, renewed,
revived, reclaimed, and redeemed and redeemed and
redeemed. Never throw out anybody.
Remember, if you ever need a helping hand,
you'll find one at the end of your arm.
As you grow older, you will discover that you have two
hands: one for helping yourself, the other for helping others.
Your "good old days" are still ahead of you,
may you have many of them.

— ©1973 Sam Levenson (this poem was loved
and often quoted by Audrey Hepburn)

FOREWORD

Woman to Woman

Women are human beings, and all human beings have worth. It is our birthright. The problem isn't whether women have value, but rather, are we valued by our families, our societies, and our nations? I do not believe that any woman has to prove her worth in order to be considered significant, but I *do* believe that women should contribute something of value to their families, their societies, and their nations. It is our duty. The reality, however, is that millions of women are hindered from fulfilling this duty because they're not given the opportunities they deserve simply because of their gender.

Society should not be questioning women's worth; society should be giving us the tools we need—adequate health care, education, and job training—to improve our lives and the lives of our children, thereby improving the condition of the society in which we live. By our nature, we're the ones who pass the values of society from one generation to another; we're the ones who teach compassion, compromise, and tolerance to the world's future leaders. This alone gives us worth.

— **Jehan Sadat,** former first lady of Egypt;
widow of former president Anwar Sadat

FOREWORD

The World of Two

Men tend to expose themselves to a greater extent than women do; hence, they are rather uniform. Women, on the other hand, are more introverted, yet every woman has her own individual personality: her hidden strength exceeds a man's manifest strength.

Women constantly shoulder responsibility; men, less so. Women shape the fate of their children—from the day they're born to the day they leave the family nest, a woman is able to deal with the challenges her offspring confront and watch over their development . . . it's an uninterrupted journey. Men stand helpless in the face of any family crisis; women instinctively marshal their inner strength to resolve the crisis. Women take on the role of educators who guide the members of the family, as they strive to create a sense of unity in the home and banish any spirit of confrontation. Men tend to scrutinize the horizon.

Women control the pulse of life. Indeed, without a robust heartbeat, it's impossible to stride forward toward new horizons. Women conceal their concern from the eyes of others; and resort to makeup, restraint, and boundless patience to that effect. Men who court women tend to forget certain vital facts: that women are their equals, and that every woman is her own person as well as being a wife, a mother, and a friend. Whoever does not grasp the wonders of women will not experience the taste of love and the significance of life as a couple.

— **Shimon Peres,** former Prime Minister of Israel, Nobel Prize laureate, and current president of Israel

PREFACE

Why Consider a Woman's Self-Worth?

A woman's sense of worth, esteem, and empowerment are essential prerequisites for a global society that purports to acquire peace, harmony, and equality. Our own feeling of self-worth should be confident and strong, solid and unshakable, equal to a man's and not questionable. End of story. Unfortunately, that's *not* the end of the story—and the story for women and girls, in fact, is *very* different from the one for boys and men. Maybe that's because *our* tale has been lost in the translation of rituals and culture over the course of time.

Is a woman's worth prescribed by society? Must women prove their worthiness? Based on the way we're generally treated, is there an unspoken message that we're less worthy than our male counterparts? At such a question, most of us become indignant and defensive and say, "Of course not!" Yet if females are equally valued and valid as individuals, why must we continually struggle for equity and a fair share of the world's bounty? While I'm sure all human beings would argue that there should *never* be an evaluation regarding our innate worth based on gender, ethnicity, or economic status, a woman's work—particularly the unpaid labor of homemaking and child rearing—is often undervalued, or not considered work at all.

Under debilitating circumstances of poverty, dependence, and illiteracy, it's a wonder that women who live in such conditions are able to form a positive view of themselves—especially since the world at large doesn't appear to support their efforts to do so. I'm generalizing, of course, but even in broad terms, the statistics regarding the status of females worldwide suggest that our story absolutely needs to change. But how can we do so? By acknowledging our unique place in life and understanding our behaviors, that's how.

I don't claim to be an authority in women's studies. I am, however, an individual who cares deeply about a woman's place in society, someone who sees our ability to use our unique voices as vital to the well-being of our children and future generations. I felt compelled to write about a woman's worth while completing my Ph.D. in psychology, although my particular focus was actually chronic illness in children.

Kids are the central focus of many women's lives, my own included. Prayers for their well-being and health are on the lips and in the hearts of females everywhere. In fact, *women and children* have very often been categorized as a unit, with the well-being and success of one affecting prospects for the other.

My interest in helping children has been lifelong, perhaps becoming galvanized in my youth when I volunteered to teach disabled boys and girls to swim. My exploration of human behavior and my desire to obtain a Ph.D. in psychology consequently stemmed from my interest in the welfare of children. I had an externship at Children's Hospital Los Angeles, where I worked with kids with cancer and other blood diseases; ironically, this experience permitted me a unique opportunity to turn my attention to moms, and by extension, all women.

The environment and temperament of a children's hospital is like no other. In a sea of heartache, parents—predominately mothers—sit for hours with their sick little ones, waiting for treatments, watching the results of treatments, and psychically bearing the pain that their children are forced to bear physically. For many of these women, resources are scant. For them to spend days on end at the hospital with one ill child means that their other family members at home aren't being attended to. Many of them are also concerned about where their next meal will come from.

I wondered how these women could cope. I have four kids, two of them still minors, but I can afford backup help, and I'm not worried about my next meal . . . or any meals in the foreseeable future, for that matter. These moms who were commuting daily to the hospital were generally (but not always) in the lower economic strata of the community—and among other things, they were struggling with an inadequate health-care system that added to their difficulties. The stress these women were under was enormous, yet I watched day after day as they carried that burden with a sense of purpose, without complaint, diligently seeking remission for their children and showing a depth of inner strength in situations that could bring most of us to our knees.

These mothers became unsung heroes for me. It's because of them that I began my research into where we stand as women; how we're valued or undervalued by society; and, more important, how we're able to develop a strong sense of self-worth despite it all.

While I'm not currently using my Ph.D. as a practicing clinical psychologist, my interest in human behavior, particularly as it relates to women and children, is unflagging. One needn't be a researcher, statistician, or academic to notice that the recognition and acknowledgment of female worth has, to some extent, been sidelined. With everything else we do—such as careers, family, marriage, and partnerships—our sense of value is often relegated to the back burner, falling far behind the needs and desires of others in our fold. Why is that? Habit? Necessity? Cultural or societal pressure?

Although I'm seeing a woman's worth through my own particular lens (one that, incidentally, is fairly rose colored), the *overall* status for women and girls is such a global problem that one of the United Nations' Millennium Development Goals for 2015 is to "Promote gender equality and empower women." Therefore, I've made a personal commitment to use my abilities, my voice, and my resources to help manifest these goals by writing essays, blogs, and articles about my fellow women, by volunteering to serve on charitable boards, by sponsoring women in war-ravaged countries, and by donating funds to organizations that promote our equality, freedom, and ability to be heard. One such organization is the International Women's Media Foundation, which supports brave female journalists all over the world; another is the Women's Funding Network, which puts money in the hands of women.

My goal with this book is to put women's expression of self-worth on the front burner—to put the importance of our validity center stage. Our collective focus will help achieve some of the UN's goals by instigating not only global *awareness,* but also global *action.* Our status and our participation in society needs to be part of an open and ongoing dialogue that is bilateral—meaning that it should take place not just in women's circles, but in *all* circles. There's no question that we've made monumental gains in some areas, but there's also no denying that we continually butt heads with antiquated traditions, fundamentalist religions, and a male-dominated mind-set. Stereotyping, typecasting, and a persistently biased attitude against the female gender exist as major stumbling blocks for us.

Such systemic resistance to women gaining equal status is true not only in developing countries, where the need for more female-centric resources is obvious, but it's also evident in the United States and other westernized societies, where we should know better. Even here in the U.S., where we take most of our rights for granted, a woman's worth and validity are routinely questioned or challenged in both subtle and unsubtle ways.

Take, for example, the disparity that persists in salaries between women and men. Even though the Equal Pay Act (EPA) passed in 1963 was meant to protect us from wage discrimination, women still earn an average of $196 per week less than men *for the same jobs.* Does this discrepancy say something about our worth? Yes, I'd say that it does. And consider the value (or lack thereof) placed on the unpaid labor of a stay-at-home mom. As long as she is married and/or being supported by others, she can go about her business. But when that support falls away, how is she to borrow on the equity of time and effort she's invested as a homemaker to continue to support her children?

I recall feeling pretty devalued myself when I first re-entered the job market after getting divorced. My skills as a homemaker and mother didn't win me any accolades, nor did they act as a stepladder to a job in human resources or office management—which I think homemakers and mothers are trained to perform by virtue of hands-on experience. Females of color, women in compromised economic circumstances, and single mothers with little outside support may feel such challenges more intensely. But even women with so-called high net worth, such as senators or presidential candidates, can find themselves defending their positions.

Knowledge empowers us; there can be *peace in understanding.* But we must also be peacefully proactive. By taking an honest look at how society views women and how we view ourselves, we may become emboldened to take action. At the very least, we'll be better prepared to empower future generations, and such empowerment is needed to bring about lasting change.

My hope is that by reading *What Is Your Self-Worth?* you'll be able to put your own sense of place in the world into better perspective, and then assume ownership. May you use this book as a guide, a flashlight in a tool kit to illuminate what you *personally* can do to ensure that you live life to your fullest potential, and thus become confident about your own worth.

INTRODUCTION

Into the Hearts
and Minds of Women

"Whatever you can do or dream you can, begin it.
Boldness has genius, power and magic in it."
— Johann Wolfgang von Goethe

The journey I began by writing *What Is Your Self-Worth?* allowed me visitation rights into the hearts and minds of hundreds of incredible women from all over the world. I found that questions about our worth loom large: Are we generally considered as worthy as men? Is everything just peachy as far as we're concerned? Have we as a gender achieved our long-sought-for equality, or do we still tend to be thought of as objects? Does the world acknowledge our substance or value? Are we second-class citizens meant to do the bidding of others? Are we given the respect and attention we deserve?

These are not new queries. Textbooks in gender-studies classes are filled with statistics and research data describing the complicated history of a woman's sense of worth and personal power. Yet although the questions aren't new, the answers aren't easy either. It seems that women continue to face the challenge of expressing and accessing a sense of self-esteem, and the answers to questions such as "How do you define your worth?" are nuanced by time, place, and culture.

As I sought to answer these questions for myself, I began to ask friends and relatives to share their opinions as well. I was so energized by the comments and emotional stories I heard that I posted a questionnaire on my Website (**www.cherylsaban.com**) and invited women from global cyberspace to participate. I was treated to a windfall of sometimes poignant but always inspiring experiences. The hundreds of replies I received came from women from several countries and ethnicities, all walks of life, and varying economic brackets; and the respondents graciously agreed to share their personal stories and insight with you.

The questions I posed to them were as follows:

- ♥ What makes a woman worthy?

- ♥ What defines your personal worth?

- ♥ Can you recall an experience in your life that really made you feel your own worth?

- ♥ What would you want the youth of today (both daughters and sons) to know about a woman's worth?

- ♥ Have you always known that you were worthwhile, or did you need to learn it to experience it; that is, to *work* for it to earn it?

Many of the revealing and thought-provoking stories I received are contained in a section at the end of each chapter of this book, under the heading "Wisdom from Your Peers." While you might recognize the names of some famous respondents, such as Jamie Lee Curtis, Diane von Fürstenberg, and Mary Steenburgen, most of the participants will be unknown to you.

As you read their comments (which have been edited for clarity), you may notice that some identifying statistics are missing, and you may think that I made a mistake or inadvertently left out pertinent information. Don't be alarmed—I'm aware of the discrepancies. The questionnaire was constructed in such a way as to allow those who replied total or partial anonymity if they so desired. While it provided an option to disclose place of birth and profession, these items weren't mandatory. Some women filled in their first names only, some stated an occupation, and others left some or all of the personal-identification lines blank.

While my research for this book doesn't fit the parameters, nor meet the standards required, for bona fide *scientific* research, the results are nevertheless compelling. It's interesting to note the profession or country of origin of some of the respondents, but it isn't necessary to appreciate the content. I guarantee that *all* of the comments and stories will resonate. You're going to read about women just like yourself, but you'll also have the chance to peer through a unique window into the experiences of those who live existences that are very different from yours. And I invite you to participate, as hundreds of other women have, by considering the questions and personal-assessment exercises that appear throughout this book.

Working with This Book

I've constructed *What Is Your Self-Worth?* to tackle the main themes or domains of a woman's life. At the end of each chapter I've included several additional segments, which essentially comprise a personal workbook—the action items for you to work on and periodically refer back to. These include:

- **Personal tasks,** which ask you to focus on specific elements of your life.

- **Wisdom from your peers,** which, as previously mentioned, are stories and comments gleaned from hundreds of women responding to my online questionnaire.

- **Journal questions,** which are a few *suggested* inquiries to jump-start your personal inquiry, help you get closer to your "inner you," and ultimately acknowledge your self-worth.

- **Self-worth affirmations,** which are a series of positive statements developed using the acronym *W.O.R.T.H.: W*isdom, *O*ptimism, *R*esponsibility, *T*enacity, and *H*onesty.

By design, there are no specific rules for the personal tasks and journal questions at the end of each chapter. I purposely interspersed the subject matter of these segments throughout the book, usually relating them to the current chapter subject, but not always. The idea is to inspire a *holistic* reflection on your part. Taking a breather at the end of each chapter to pause and reflect on conditions of worth, as well as on your life experiences thus far, is an important part of the overall experience of this book.

It's important that you take the time to write down your thoughts and investigate your feelings in a journal (feel free to use the one I've provided on my Website, or you can purchase one yourself). As many women have shared with me, the exercise of putting pen to paper is surprisingly fulfilling and personally revealing. How you answer these questions for yourself may inspire a new perspective for you; after all, your life *is* a personal journey.

Although you might find yourself struggling with the answers to the questions I pose about worth, do yourself a favor and ponder them anyway. What *is* your personal currency? I'll explain the context within which I use currency in more detail in later chapters, but to be clear, please note that I'm not referring to a monetary equivalent for who you are; instead, I'd like to know the sense of power, esteem, and validity you assign to *yourself.* Your personal currency is what you use to move about in this world—it's how you relate to others, along with how you impact the environment you function in.

Recognition and awareness of your own worth, innate value, and potential will help you align with the greater collective. Such a group effort will give rise to a new global mind-set that *promotes and celebrates* women rather than stratifies, stereotypes, and oppresses us. The goal for this collaboration and the wisdom of our collective experience is to illuminate those suppressed and obscured facets of our individual identities—*our essence.* In other words, let's work together to reveal the worth that's there, whether the light is on or not.

Ultimately, this book is a testimony to the endurance of women. It's part recovery, part guidance system, and part journal, with the end result being a sense of satisfaction. *We know what we're worth, and each and every one of us has the ability to define, expose, and append what that is.*

Now it's up to you to pass the torch. Your female friends and family members need to understand that they are worthwhile and valuable because of who and what they are *inside.* And the men in your life need to get this message, too. It is long overdue.

The material within these pages is meant to provide at least three things: a window, a breeze, and a set of wings. The window is for you to look through—both forward and back—to visualize what you and I and other women like us have done, said, and felt about the subject of our worth and where such disclosures might lead. This window is a safe vantage point: you can view a few episodes of my personal saga and witness what many other female predecessors have experienced without tumbling onto the same rocky section of the road.

The breeze is to calm your soul; to refresh your memory of the moments in time that most exhilarated you—those profound experiences that caused you to breathe in satisfaction. This metaphorical breeze is there to elevate you, fill you with more oxygen, awaken you, lift you up, and perhaps even free you.

The set of wings is whimsical, but imagine them anyway. Use them to fly through your memories; to make peace with your past; and to take a broader, more global look at your life. Humor yourself, and allow your wings to take you where *you* want to go. Use the questions posed in these pages to flesh out your inner feelings—to become the historian of the life you've chosen. As you fly, no matter when or where you embarked on your own travels, remember to tell yourself how *worth it* you are . . . because baby, *you* are the one who's in charge of establishing it, and *you* are the one who needs to endorse it and project it.

Women from all over the world described to me what worth means to them—how they realize it, achieve it, wish for it, or find it. Women of all ages, from all walks of life, and from all socioeconomic backgrounds have a say in the collective definition of female worth, and though it's clear that we've generally been defined by a male-dominated zeitgeist, the truth about our worth prevails. Every single one of us has a stake in redefining it—we decide the narrative we're going to share and then leave behind.

The truth about self-worth essentially distills down to a sense of personal currency—that is, personal power, personal responsibility, and personal respect. Within these pages you'll find the path; the method; the criteria; and the syllabus for assessing, projecting, and celebrating your own worth. Heed it. Own it. Do it.

We women must take our seats at the proverbial roundtable, for we'll need to be an equal part of society's dialogue in order to achieve that status. Perhaps then, when the truth about our worth and validity is out of the bag, we'll finally be able to persuade our global society to *grow up.*

"Knowing others is wisdom,
knowing yourself is enlightenment."
— **Lao-tzu**

PART I

Assessing: How Do We Define a Woman's Worth?

"We are all born worthy. Worthy of love, worthy of success."
— **Jamie Lee Curtis;** mother, actor,
writer, activist; California

"I feel like women have the same standards for worthiness as men: commitment to a high level of personal and civic responsibility, interest in the human beings you share your space with (near and far), and a felicity of self that can be expressed creatively or spiritually. We do have one added responsibility: to continue the work of feminism in some way, and that can mean any number of things."
— **Shauna McKenna;** Minnesota

"What makes a woman worthy is her strength, her courage, and her telling her truth. Also, her ability to show her strength, love, and care to her surroundings, including herself."
— **Zainab Salbi;** founder and CEO,
Women for Women International; Iraq

*"What makes a woman worthy? Every human has worth.
I think first of my humanity, rather than my womanhood,
to feel worthy. Although the world has sometimes invited
me to, I have never for one moment felt 'less than' for having
been privileged to be born a woman. I take joy in the fact
that I have brought two children into the world and nurtured
them and two stepdaughters with all my heart. I delight
in my 'femininity,' which includes my stubbornness, my
flexibility, my ambition, and my laissez-faire. I never apologize
for my age. I like being the age that I am. I feel more worthy
as a 54-year-old woman than I ever did in my youth.
And that's a good thing. I don't want my daughters to
fear growing older. I want to be an example to them of
a life fully lived and embraced with pride."*
— **Mary Steenburgen;**
actor, activist, human being; Arkansas

CHAPTER 1

Taking Inventory:
Recognition and Responsibility

*"The whole theory of the universe is directed unerringly
to one single individual—namely to You."*
— from *Leaves of Grass,* by **Walt Whitman**

What is your personal currency? What do you feel you have to offer to the world at large—and is that offering given the value, validity, and respect it deserves? Are you happy to be a female? When you judge yourself, as we all do, how do you measure up? Are you an equally treasured part of society? Are you predictable? Does being a woman ever make you feel compromised in any way? When you consider your worth as a woman, what comes to mind? This subject may expose emotions and responses that surprise you.

For example, what are the rulers or measuring tools you use? Do you think of:

- Your marriage?
- Your ability to provide for your children?
- Your success in the workplace?
- Your friendships and family relationships?
- Your hobbies and avocations?
- Your sense of well-being and fulfillment?

- Your dedication to helping others?
- Your faith?

Do you even consider *your* worth at all? Perhaps not in so many words, but the subject of worthiness or validity probably comes up for you time and again, and it's manifested by behaviors and gender stereotypes that don't serve you well. Does the idea of objectification conjure up significant images for you? (Think *sexual plaything, object,* and so on.) How about gender stereotypes? Have you ever found yourself automatically identifying with words such as *weak, frail,* or *defenseless?* Such adjectives are often used to describe women.

We live in an era when we're obsessed with obsession—a psychological disorder in which individuals become fixated on an often unreasonable idea or feeling, or a perceived or imaginary defect in the way they look; so eating disorders, obesity, obsessive-compulsive disorders, and body dysmorphic disorders all fall into this category. Are we making the grave mistake of using such disordered thinking to regulate our overall perception of self-worth? Do we associate thinness with perfection or consider variations in body type as flaws? When we take into consideration that nearly ten million females in the United States are struggling with eating disorders, we may begin to wonder. . . .

Are we incapable of setting our own standards? Misconceptions and maladaptations to outside *and* inside influences can infantilize us into a state of helplessness. The "Cinderella complex" (a theory first described by Colette Dowling in her 1981 book of the same name) suggests that women actually *fear* independence and have an unconscious desire to be taken care of.

While it's possible that some of us have been pre-programmed with this particular mind-set, *helpless* is not the word I'd use to describe most women I know, nor should you be willing to attach that descriptor to yourself. However, do be aware that such an unconscious desire may indeed have been included in the bag of tricks you were given as a youngster, and it could invade your behavior when you least expect it. Here's an important note for you to jot down in your personal journal or diary: *resist it.* Play to your strengths, not your weaknesses. Confidence is your best asset, but it's also your most attractive fashion lure, if that's a consideration for you.

Why is it important to understand your true value or personal currency? I'm going to be bold and say that not only is it important to recognize your innate worth, it's *critical* that you do. Your survival and sense of well-being virtually depend upon it.

Discovering the Meaning of <u>Worth</u>

What does *worth* mean to you? How do you define or assess it? Is there a general measurement of it that holds true for everyone? Most likely, you've formed a conception of what *self-worth* and *self-esteem* are, but for the sake of clarity, it might be helpful to analyze these terms. We use them so often that their meaning may have lost potency.

According to the highly regarded *Oxford American Dictionary*, *worth* means "sufficiently good, important, or interesting to justify a specified action." The thesaurus includes these synonyms: *merit, value, excellence, caliber, quality, stature, eminence, importance, significance,* and *distinction.* Such words help synthesize what can be tricky to define in a finite way.

The following list of terms may help illuminate the concept even further:

- *Self-esteem:* the value, respect, and honor you have for yourself

- *Conditions of worth:* the do's and don'ts, shoulds and shouldn'ts, that you live by in order to feel appreciated and accepted by others

- *Self-concept:* the organized set of perceptions and ideas you have for yourself

- *Self-actualization:* a principle of human behavior stating that you strive to develop your capacities and talents to the fullest—that is, growing and enhancing the basic self

- *Self-efficacy:* your expectation that you can effectively cope with and master situations, as well as bring about desired outcomes through personal efforts

- *Social stratification:* the ranking of individuals into groups within a culture

- *Resilience:* being able to withstand, or recover quickly from, difficult conditions

So how *do* you feel about yourself? Are you your number one fan? Do you flounder along in blind acceptance of other people's rules?

Keep in mind that our culture and environment typically stipulate markers or benchmarks for the establishment of mastery and validity. While such markers often provide the context for viability by measuring specific aptitude and/or ability for a particular undertaking (such as entrance to medical school), in other cases, cultural rituals and habits serve no greater purpose than to control our behavior. "Groupthink," peer pressure, and media messages all exploit our vulnerabilities; and they can also coerce us to believe that we're not beautiful, smart, or worthwhile unless we conform to a specific mind-set.

Take a moment now to let your mind float away from the culturally induced markers for validity you've been subjected to. Can you resist the incessant outside editing and altering that society subjects you to and see the incredible person you are inside? Can you *feel* validated and valued? Will you grant yourself that level of respect? Understand that when you recognize your innate worth, you're more inclined to strive to fulfill your potential, and having done that, you *will* be happy.

Women who are successful exude a sense of confidence *in themselves.* One of the things such individuals have in common is their ability to harness their own thoughts and behaviors; they bring a great deal of personal intention to their lives. They realize that they're the directors of their own destinies and therefore take a positive stance as they look forward. They're *happy* people—by happy, I'm referring to an experience of contentment, joy, or positive well-being. It's the sense that life is generally good, meaningful, and worthwhile.

Are you in that place? Do you think you can create that kind of life for yourself? Specialists in the field of psychology and behavior say that you can. Armed with the wisdom and reflections of hundreds of women who responded to my questionnaire about their worth, I will show you how.

The first step in acknowledging and accessing your worth, value, and sense of fulfillment is to take an honest *personal assessment.* Set aside some quiet time where you can have privacy and think.

Now take out your journal and a pen, and answer the following questions:

- ♥ Are you happy?
- ♥ What gives you joy?
- ♥ What contributions do you make?
- ♥ Do you feel acknowledged for these contributions?
- ♥ Are your relationships fulfilling?
- ♥ Do you nurture and enjoy your relationships?
- ♥ Are you achieving goals that you set for yourself?
- ♥ Do your activities and lifestyle contribute to your sense of worth and well-being?
- ♥ Do you take personal responsibility for your actions?
- ♥ Does something or someone else dictate how you should feel or act?

If you don't want to write down answers to these questions, at least consider them. And feel free to add additional queries of your own that are more specific to the particulars in *your* life.

An assessment of who you are and where you stand is vital to your ability to function freely in the world. Be creative, and assess yourself with *flair*. Does this sound frivolous to you? It shouldn't, for it's a joyful recognition of who you are. By evaluating and recognizing your abilities, you validate yourself, and you need to be able to do that before anyone else can validate you.

I've gone over all of the questions on the previous page myself, and I admit that the first few responses I wrote were brief and short on details. But as I allowed myself more time to think, I began to remember things about my life, along with how I truly feel about particular memories. My personal assessments and soul- searching answers to difficult questions have helped me get to know myself. The journal I've written all of this in has become my own never-ending story, and for me, it's a treasure.

FYI, when you assess and validate yourself, you're accepting the truth about who you are. This is not a form of surrender, although your insecure mind may take you to that conclusion temporarily. Please resist that. Accept your assessment as *intentional recognition*—which actually sounds more like power and self-determination than surrender. When you can accept yourself as an individual, you become even more credible as a participant in the collective.

Own It!

Assessing your life demands a certain level of pride, respect, and courage because it means you're taking responsibility for it. Responsibility also suggests ownership—of your feelings and actions, as well as the *outcomes* of your actions. The easiest road may *not* be your chosen path, and growing pains *will* be part of your overall development. Nobody said life and growth would be easy.

It's a good idea to learn to take responsibility at a young (that is, eager and absorbent) age. So if you're a mother, I hope you'll teach your children to be independent and self-assured when they're still little. Give them opportunities to work out their problems, which includes allowing them to fail occasionally so that they can figure out for themselves how to succeed. It takes courage to let your kids individuate away from you—but trust me, they'll benefit, and you'll feel a sense of accomplishment as well.

Individuation is a psychological term used to describe when individuals separate or distinguish themselves from others, and it's a big part of personal discovery. We've all done it—it's a natural, yet sometimes difficult, transition. If we have teenagers, we know how this feels, and we can be certain our mothers felt the same way.

When cultures, rituals, and customs establish constraints to it, individuating can be especially tricky. For example, in various parts of the world, females are continually stratified and marginalized: Many women are relegated to roles and duties prescribed by antiquated cultural mores and rules that make life difficult, arduous, and at times seemingly hopeless. Girls are routinely denied education, ownership rights, and power over their bodies. So the suggestion that they buck the system and take charge of their lives may seem as disingenuous as telling them to fly like birds.

Yet stories continually surface of women in dire, restrictive circumstances who manage to take action to change their lives for the better despite the odds against them. One notable example is Ayaan Hirsi Ali, who so eloquently shares her personal saga in her book *Infidel.*

Born in Mogadishu, Somalia, Ali has dared to criticize Islam, a defiance that could cost her her life. Her screenplay for Theo Van Gogh's movie *Submission,* which criticizes the position of women in Islamic societies, resulted in death threats against her. (Van Gogh himself was murdered in 2004 by a Muslim.) Despite the very real dangers facing Ali, and perhaps in spite of her upbringing as an obedient Muslim daughter, she's become an outspoken advocate for women and a political activist. Even though she now lives and works in an undisclosed location in the Netherlands, her story as recounted in *Infidel* reveals her deep convictions and unfaltering courage. Read it and weep . . . Ayaan Hirsi Ali is a true hero.

Your ambitions and goals are not that dissimilar from women in other cultures. While your everyday circumstances may differ, you can still find your own courage. No matter your age, think of yourself as the director and producer of your life, rather than the adjunct player in someone else's. *Own* your place on the planet. Consider what would be good *for you* for a change.

In concrete ways, when you own your worth, you honor women everywhere, and the trickle-down effect of your actions will ultimately reach every corner of the globe. As part of your personal inventory and assessment, give some thought to the following exercises, and write down the answers in your journal:

- ♥ **List your current duties and obligations** (such as being a personal consultant, mother, wife, caretaker of aging parents, chef, house manager, and accountant).

- ♥ **List your life goals** (for example, to climb Mount Everest, to become a partner in your law firm, to raise happy and healthy children, and to have a fulfilling relationship).

- ♥ **Describe your innate abilities or talents** (which come through in the hobbies you like to do and the activities you excel at—perhaps including good people skills, a positive attitude, a knack for organizing, and patience).

- ♥ **Identify what stands in the way of achieving your goals.**

- ♥ **Consider new steps you can take to enhance your abilities and learn new skills.**

Without personal awareness of your abilities, goals, and challenges, you might lose sight of your choices. When you fight the urge to accept out of hand what society dictates, you'll experience an enormous sense of freedom. You *do* have options in life; you just need to be willing to use them.

Turning on Your Light

Women are just as inherently worthy, valuable, and valid as men are, but our *possession* of this reality can be more tenuous than it is for our male counterparts. That's because we've been raised within a cultural mind-set that defines gender-specific roles and modes of behavior that prescribe how we should act, whether those actions are beneficial for us or not.

As an aside, although I often refer to the dominant male mind-set, this journey is not about male bashing; I *love* men. Just like you, I have several men in my life whom I adore. The quest for substantiation is not about blame or revenge.

At any rate, please think of this expedition you're embarking upon more in terms of *an awakening,* a turning on of your light. This is an invitation for you to recognize, validate, and *apply* your full potential in all domains of your life. The truth is, you can't begin to change the way society responds to you until you're clear about what you want that response to be. So check yourself out: how do you measure up, not to societal dictates, but on your own achievement scale?

It's time to take a cue from strong women who have resisted a narrow-minded vision: take responsibility for your self-worth. Define your personality by stipulating your *own* style, fashion statement, and boundaries. Get a little insight about how you feel by performing a stream-of-thought exercise that itemizes the wonderful, positive things about yourself. When you've got a mental list of positive statements that pertain to the many domains of your life, write them down.

For example, you might start with the following:

- ♥ I'm married to a man I love.
- ♥ I'm a mother, and I feel fulfilled and blessed in this role.
- ♥ I work full-time and share financial obligations in my household.
- ♥ My partner and I are happy and healthy, and we greatly enjoy spending time together.
- ♥ I have parents who love me.
- ♥ I get along with my siblings.
- ♥ My career is interesting and stimulating.
- ♥ I love to ski, and I find fulfillment in developing that skill.
- ♥ I exercise at least three times a week and enjoy feeling energized.
- ♥ I love to read and cook, but I also feel happy when I learn something new.
- ♥ I love volunteering and helping others. It makes me feel good to give back.

Your positive statements can be about anything and everything you do and/or are involved with. The exercise is valuable because your assessment will help you reconnect with your authentic self and establish personal integrity. Define actions going forward that are appropriate for *you*. By knowing who you are and what you're capable of, you'll suddenly stand up straighter; breathe more deeply; and feel more secure, productive, and alive. It's an amazing feeling.

Strengthen Your Core

Honest, in-depth personal knowledge is called "insight." This is a deep, intuitive understanding of yourself that strengthens your core—the place inside of you that your yoga teacher talks about. Your core needs to be both strong and resilient in order to handle the tectonic shifts your world surprises you with. Happy, successful women nurture this inner part of themselves because they know that when they radiate an aura of strength, the people around them feel safer, too.

Such calm, resolute energy is attractive, a turn-on. You'll receive instant feedback, since projecting a positive sense of strength makes people want to be around you. *Aha!* This, then, is an important lesson to learn: when the people you care about are safe, secure, and happy, a mutually beneficial circle is created around you as well. Your sense of self-esteem increases, a sense of autonomy occurs, and confidence blooms.

Begin your process of self-evaluation now by spending some one-on-one time with numero uno—yourself. Find a quiet corner and allocate some precious time to discovering *you.* Try for 30 minutes a day, but even 15 minutes will get you started. Let yourself stare into space, think, dream, ponder. . . .

Okay, I'm sure that some of you are wondering, *What's she smoking? Who has the luxury of extra, disposable time?* While it's true that so many of us have overscheduled ourselves to the point of exhaustion, consequently leaving very little time in our lives for staring into space and reflection, the time we make for ourselves is *quality* time that not only do we need, we deserve.

Utilize all your formidable multitasking skills to carve out some time for yourself. When you drive home after taking the kids to school, for instance, do some soul-searching along the way. Repeat positive affirmations at stoplights, or take that time to pray. I spend time with myself when I work out on the treadmill or cross-training machines in the gym. This is a great time to get into a "thinking about myself" zone. In fact, I often come up with some of my best writing while I'm walking on the treadmill.

Whatever you do, even if you just hide in your bathroom for ten minutes a day, breathe deeply and give yourself the gift of positive rumination. Think of yourself in the best possible way, and choose to do whatever you can to enhance the quality of your life *today*.

Personal Tasks

Take inventory of your personal currency by completing the following exercise: write down an honest assessment of your abilities, attributes, and current goals.

Here are some examples to get you started:

- ♥ I'm a people person.
- ♥ I have a good sense of humor.
- ♥ I don't feel confident about money.
- ♥ I'm an excellent skier.
- ♥ I'm a loving, accommodating spouse.
- ♥ I make kick-ass chili.
- ♥ I'm a great mother.
- ♥ I'm insecure about speaking my mind.
- ♥ I play the cello.

- ♥ I'm currently learning a new language.
- ♥ I want to continue my education.
- ♥ I'm nurturing.
- ♥ I feel overwhelmed sometimes, but I handle it.
- ♥ I'm kind.

Now frame your abilities, attributes, and goals within the context of your self-worth and happiness:

- ♥ I feel worthwhile when I _____.
- ♥ I'm competent and successful in my _____.
- ♥ I'm happiest when I _____.
- ♥ My achievements make me feel worthwhile because _____.
- ♥ I'm strongest when I _____.
- ♥ My positive outlook for my future includes _____.
- ♥ My friends and relatives appreciate me for my
  _____.
- ♥ I like myself because I'm _____.
- ♥ I feel fulfilled and confident when _____.

Continue to develop your personal inventory/assessment/ evaluation because it's a fluid exercise. It's also entirely worth every moment you spend on it: by paying attention to the things that matter to *you,* you'll make discoveries about inner strengths and passions that have been in hiding for much too long, and reveal options and opportunities you may not have believed were there. Open the door, turn on the light, and expose your inner self.

Wisdom from Your Peers

"I believe a woman is only as worthy as the value she places on herself. We all have gifts, but for some reason it's customary to deny or reject these gifts. It's a shame to live in such denial for so many years, for age catches up with you— and if you don't recognize the talents in yourself that you wish others would legitimize, no one will. If you don't value your own worth, no one else ever will. It's baffling to me that men are raised to be confident and self-assured. Women must overcome the unsavory notion our culture has instilled in us to be humble. It's seen as arrogant or conceited to have the very same qualities that are valued in men. I suppose we are more fragile by nature, but somehow I can't ever get past the notion of inequity in this respect. Perhaps our ultimate revenge for such an eternal 'glass ceiling' would be our unique ability to procreate. This is something a boy can never achieve. . . ."
— **Athena Helbing,** retail-store manager, Colorado

"My teenage years were the hardest in terms of my self-worth, which I'm sure is the case with many women. It's such an awkward stage, and kids can be so cruel. I began to discover that the best way to deal with my low-self-esteem issues was to set goals for myself and strive to achieve them. With every goal I attained, I began to feel more self-confident and secure. It's something I still subscribe to in my personal and professional life, and it helps me be a more productive, healthy person."
— **Julie Ashton,** casting director, Ohio

18

"I think the most important thing for a woman to remember is that true worth comes from within—not from what others think of us, but from what we think of ourselves."
—Trish Ploehn, child-welfare director, New Jersey

"Having children has had a profound impact on my sense of self-worth. I became far more aware of my personal endurance, flexibility, intuitiveness, creativity, and patience. I have never felt more worthy than when I care for my children's development, education, and welfare. However, even though having children helped to clarify my worthiness, that alone certainly does not define one's worth."
— Ann Soh Woods, home management, Illinois

Journal Questions

- What specific attribute, characteristic, or "fact" about yourself gives you a feeling of worth?

- How can you make yourself feel better today?

- What do you do to make sure you honor the work you do in your home?

- What makes you laugh, smile, and feel joy? What are you doing to make sure that you experience those sensations every day of your life?

Self-Worth Affirmations

W.O.R.T.H.
Wisdom
I gain confidence by continuing
to gain knowledge.

W.O.R.T.H.
Optimism
I establish attainable
financial goals.

W.O.R.T.H.
Responsibility
I keep learning, reading, growing,
and changing.

W.O.R.T.H.
Tenacity
I maximize my skill set. I increase
my current skills.

W.O.R.T.H.
Honesty
I tell myself happy stories and write
about what I am grateful for.

CHAPTER 2

Basic Training: Sorting Out the Mixed Messages

*"Expecting the world to treat you fairly because you are
a good person is a little like expecting a bull not to
attack you because you are a vegetarian."*
— **Dennis Wholey,** producer, author, and television host

Every human being is raised by parents or caregivers who endowed him or her with specific "rules of the road." With that in mind, how were *you* brought up? Think about the following questions:

- ♥ How did you learn to be the person you are?

- ♥ How do you define yourself as an individual?

- ♥ How do you suppose your perceptions of what it means to be female were formed?

- ♥ Do you believe that there's a particular prescription passed out to parents of girls that's different from the one given to parents of boys?

- ♥ Did you grow up with choices and a balanced view of the world?

♥ Did you feel empowered or restricted because of your gender?

♥ Were you instilled with a sense of entitlement, or were you denied one?

Looking at my own life, I realize that I had no sense of what women outside my own community were like when I was a little girl. The world at large—including other societies and cultures and females' place in them—was as unreal and one-dimensional to me as the scant photos or drawings I'd seen in schoolbooks. My exposure to anything or anyone outside of my narrow vision of life was basically nil. My family and I lived in a neighborhood of similar cookie-cutter homes three blocks from my grammar school, one block from our church, and two blocks from the bus stop that my father walked to every morning to commute to work. Although we had a car that my dad drove on weekends, my mom didn't start driving until I was eight or nine years old. Television, which was relatively new and still quite precious at that time, didn't offer the kind of window on the world that media provides now. My perspective of life was basically formed by what I saw and experienced within a one-mile radius.

Because it was the 1950s, I was easily branded by the notion of what girls "should" and "should not" do. Likewise, the history curriculum I was taught in school didn't spend much time focusing on the contributions of women—who, for the most part, were solely mentioned in the context of the famous men they were "helping." And to be perfectly honest, those few ladies who received their own pages in the history books of my early childhood didn't seem real to me, since they weren't like the people I knew. These women were mysterious, foreign, and untouchable; therefore, they didn't play a big part in molding my youthful ideas about gender roles.

Of course, as I grew older and became exposed to more worldly news, I was better able to absorb the historical proof that women were much more multifaceted in scope than what I was privy to. I was then able to look through a window on life that afforded multiple views. But by that time in my development, my basic training had pretty much accomplished what it was meant to: my impression of what was expected of me as a girl and then as a woman was indelibly embedded in my mind.

To this day, I still connect women and mothering to nurturing and the sustenance of life. This core essence, which goes well beyond my childhood visions, sticks with me as one of the essential abilities females bring to the table and remains deep inside me as part of who I am.

But over the course of my life, I've learned that the nurturing, cooking, cleaning, and helping parts of me make up a very small percentage of who I am. My worth can't be described or prescribed merely by the roles society deems I should play. (And please note that I state this without casting slurs or denigrating those roles in any way.) My innate worth is existential, and in some ways, defies explanation.

So what has *your* experience been like? Did your basic training open your mind to possibilities, or did it reinforce prescribed boundaries that kept you in your "place"? Either way, I'm sure you'll agree that the realization and acceptance of the fact that all women have innate worth, which goes far beyond the stereotypes we've been raised on, is a vital lesson— even though, sadly, it's not one that's universally taught.

It's critical that you see yourself for who you are and what you're capable of, since this brings you face-to-face with your potential and your ability to actualize it. I hope your parents helped you learn this nurturing lesson as you were growing up; if they did, I further hope that you've been able to sustain that inner feeling of worth and confidence.

But for too many of us, the lesson went untaught or was sidelined . . . or even worse, it was hijacked by a different mind-set. Our potential, our ability to be counted as equal participants in life—our *self-worth*—isn't a subject to be debated. Nor should it be distilled through societal rules that attempt to brand us, control us, or bend us to its double-standard-skewed will. And if I could impose a fairness doctrine, I'd make sure that it didn't take a lifetime for girls to discover their worth, value, legitimacy, and validity. Unfortunately, too often that's just what happens.

The Prevalence of Mixed Messages

Life isn't particularly fair. The truth of that statement is underscored by the staggeringly lopsided statistics on the global status of females, which show that our basic training is flawed and needs to evolve.

Women educators and the feminists of our day are studying the impact of a predominantly male-oriented mind-set and how such omnipresent restrictions of thought affect young college coeds. It turns out that many girls seeking higher learning find it difficult to be heard through the testosterone-fueled "white noise" of their surroundings. Don't you find this surprising? Hello—this means they don't feel that their voices are loud enough, strong enough, valid enough, or all of the above.

Just so we're clear, I'm talking about *today's* young women, most of whom are computer literate, are well versed in the Internet, have Facebook and MySpace accounts, can access any piece of information they need in seconds, and have the ability to study virtually any curriculum their hearts desire. College kids today are not exactly out of the loop, as it were. From the outside looking in, I would have guessed these young women to be more aggressive, since they seem to be bold, confident, and empowered to me. Yet they report feeling stifled, and in some cases, dominated.

The ubiquitous testosterone-fueled background chatter continues to supersede our attempts at a heterogeneous information highway. Amazing, isn't it? But then again, perhaps it isn't—especially when we consider that many of the rituals, cultural schemas, and rules (including the lion's share of college curricula that inform our conduct in society) were initially *devised* by men. These same men often set up such guidelines with very little thought given to our perspective, sense of place, or well-being.

And consider the following:

- Men are seen as authority figures; masculinity is associated with strength, knowledge, and ability.

- Females are considered vulnerable, gentle, meek, and in need of protection.

- Women are associated with fashion, sex, children, and relationships.

♥ The gender bias is evident in many careers, including aviation. Even though Madame Thérèse Peltier became the first woman to fly an airplane solo in 1908, it wasn't until 1973 that a woman, Captain Emily Warner, was finally hired by a U.S. scheduled airline.

You may not be aware of these underlying influences, since you've been raised within the cocoon of them all your life. Frankly, men aren't generally aware of them either; after all, male-centric viewpoints have been in place for hundreds of years, maybe more. But when college girls today state that they find it difficult to express their opinions or stand up to male attitudes, it's clear something's *gotta* give.

We live in a century when not only do women vote and hold high-level political offices, but half of the female population is in the workforce, and 65 percent of our educators are women. With so many historical gains, what is it that causes thoroughly modern students to be reluctant to speak up?

Such disinclination to vocalize an opinion can be explained at least in part by the sometimes subtle and sometimes blatant mixed messages society continues to send about what it means to be a woman, as well as the value (or lack of it, as the case may be) assigned to a woman's voice.

Consider your primal indoctrination to society, and the specific messages you were given. Keep in mind the way girls and boys are guided into specific tracks right at the starting line:

- Childhood books depict girls baking pies, while boys drive tractors.

- Movies and television portray young women as being "boy crazy" or obsessed with relationships, while young men are portrayed as "playing the field" or more into cars and sports than commitment.

- From infancy, clothing and other items are color coded for girls—from soft, gentle, pastel pink to buck-the-system feisty red. As for boys, their infant clothing is styled in light blues and greens, but then it quickly graduates to bold, bright, and *strong* primary colors.

Even though we women are continually stretching against our boundaries, attempting to eradicate discrimination between the sexes, changing the discriminatory mind-set has proven to be significantly more difficult. Gender-specific messages are ubiquitous, and not merely in early childhood representations. Such generalizations and a gender-specific agenda are present in many domains of life, including the social sciences. Now, I'm not suggesting that we should refute them, but are you aware that most psychological theories and interventions are male oriented?

What I'm referring to here is the practice of basing research and theoretical observations solely on the evaluations of men, and then using those concepts, evaluations, and observations to diagnose female behaviors and conditions. The inclination of developmental theorists to project a masculine image can be traced at least to Freud, but he wasn't alone in his bias. Take a look around: that bias pops up in sports, journalism, science, politics, and more. In fact, it can be very helpful to examine the messages society as a whole sends to boys and girls.

Boys are raised to believe that they're:

- Leaders
- Number one
- Top of the food chain
- Entitled
- Okay as they are
- Stronger, smarter, and more clever

In addition, they're taught that:

- Negotiation is part of life; it's a challenge, a game to be won.

- It isn't a personal failure if they're turned down; on the contrary, it's motivation to try a different tactic next time.

Girls, on the other hand, are taught to believe that they're:

- Soft and pliable
- Gentle and kind
- Nurturing to others
- Service oriented
- Compliant, obedient, and patient
- Destined to be mothers and wives
- Physically weaker than men are, so they need men to protect them

In addition, they're (unfortunately) taught that:

- There is a pecking order.
- Their strengths are not always appreciated.
- Their weaknesses can be exploited.

At the end of the day, the ever-present, male-centric background noise that we women function within reinforces the fact that we're continually being measured using a male's yardstick, which explains why we're not always a perfect fit.

Learning to Speak Up

The aforementioned research about voice reveals a deep-seated vulnerability among college-aged women. It suggests that women are growing up with a reluctance to use our voices, and in some cases, we're afraid to take a stand. Ladies, believe it or not, we're inadvertently being socialized with internal and external barriers that hamper our ability to speak freely, not only in social settings or with those in perceived authority, but in our personal relationships as well.

My own "Aha!" moment on this subject occurred when I signed up to work with a speech coach to ramp up for a speaking tour. I discovered that at some point in my early life, I'd donned an emotional muzzle. That muzzle, which was invisible to all including me, was surprisingly effective.

The first day I worked with this coach, I froze while standing on a small stage that was rigged with lights to simulate a speaking engagement. Just to be sure you understand the circumstances, I was facing not hundreds of people, but one person. *One guy.* Yes, he was a professional in his field, but *I'm* a professional in my field, too. So that couldn't have been it.

While I stood on that stage, awkwardly seeking a comfortable position, I got stiff and a knot formed in my chest that moved up to my throat. I became rooted to the floor like a tree and became tighter, more compact—smaller by the moment. I'm 5'8", yet I'd condensed myself into the space a Chihuahua would have been cramped in. Not knowing where to put my hands and unsure of what to say, I felt my body go into a fight-or-flight sequence. I stopped breathing, and my heart was thumping so hard I thought I'd pass out. I tried to speak, but my words caught in my throat. I actually swallowed them rather than express myself. You can imagine how bizarre this situation was, and perhaps you can sense how I felt as I stood there freaking out in front of an audience of one.

Looking back now, I can see what was going on. At that cathartic moment onstage, my mind became flooded with long-buried memories of dealings with men that had been unpleasant, unfair, and abusive. Without going into specifics, I will say that one of those memories included the horrifying experience of being raped, and the humiliating way I was treated by police investigators when I reported it.

Those suppressed memories hit me hard. I had no idea I still harbored unresolved fears of stating my case, of telling my truth. But here—in body language and a closed throat—was proof positive that I did. Big time.

The speech coach who'd been observing my strange transformation onstage told me that I needed to find my voice, that I needed to give myself permission to be heard.

Permission! Can you imagine? I thought this a very odd suggestion at the time, since I was alone on the stage and had paid for my lesson. Permission for what?

Yet when I pondered the experience later, permission was exactly what I thought I lacked. On that fateful day, my coach didn't know what mental movie I was playing in my mind; nevertheless, he gave me an intervention that pulled me out of my past. He *connected* me to my voice. He had me focus on my air, my breathing, my throat, my abdomen, and my core. He gave me a directive to project my voice to the back wall. In fact, he had me shout, multiple times, "It's okay to hear my voice!" And it was mind-blowing.

After a few shouts, my voice actually did become clear and strong. The stranglehold grip of my fears abated, and I felt a release. The coach told me that my voice was beautiful. *Oh my God . . .* I almost had to scrape myself off the floor.

I highly recommend practicing the exercise my coach gave me whenever you feel wimpy, weak, or voiceless. At the very least, it will get you breathing again—and even better, it will make you laugh.

Here are a few more suggestions to un-muzzle and *use* your beautiful voice:

— **Allow yourself to take up space.** Take possession of that stage you're on. Do a visual inventory of the room, and then give yourself permission to be there.

— **Breathe!** Take five to ten deep, full breaths before you speak. You'll be amazed how this simple action grounds you, but at the same time it gives you wings (and clarity).

— **Know that your voice is beautiful.** It's okay to hear it, so project! Aim for the back of the room. This doesn't mean you need to shout; simply speak as if you're *entitled* to.

— **Establish an anchor.** Train yourself to think of happy moments, beautiful sights, and personal triumphs; then play this mental movie to yourself before you go onstage, enter the boardroom, or speak to your boss.

The Best Way to Negotiate

As you can see, underlying insecurity and perceived mental shackles (which are a reflection of past experiences, societal rules, and cultural rituals) can keep you from negotiating better deals and a better *life* for yourself. Hanging on to faulty logic and habitual behaviors that keep you subdued, reluctant, or silent will make your negotiation position weak at best.

Many women assume that if we do a fantastic job—that is, if we're "good" and follow directions well—we'll get our fair share. There's this *kind and fair* logic that comes into play for most of us, and we believe that our boss will simply realize how wonderful we are, congratulate us, and offer us the big raise or benefits we deserve. Sorry to tell you this, but it ain't so. If we want a better deal, we need to lobby for it *ourselves.* Just ask any female executive, and she'll back up this claim.

When I look back at my own track record, I admit that I wish I'd learned negotiating skills *before* I went back to work as a secretary-cum-office manager at a design firm so many years ago that it seems like a past life now. My boss was a friend, and he'd done me a favor by hiring me . . . and he knew it. This made for a very weak position for negotiation. Consequently, I was never able to gain a foothold on my self-esteem in that particular job. The lesson to be learned here? *Know your own worth.* And even if you don't really believe in it, buck up and state it anyway.

Note that men have no problem negotiating for themselves, and they don't let their emotions trip them out about it either. Why? Because they've been raised to believe that they're tough enough to handle challenges. Well, guess what? So are we.

Learn from your male counterparts. When you think it's time to reevaluate your salary or increase your remuneration for something, go for broke and ask for what you *really* deserve, and see what happens. You may not get the full raise this time, but you'll send a powerful message to your boss that you know you're worth it. Remember the old saying "no guts, no glory"? Well, it's true. Even for girls.

Yet how do you combat something as enmeshed in your psyche as evolution and your upbringing? By using what's beneficial for you. It's called "selective adaptation": *select* those behaviors that are needed for survival, and *adapt* the ones that don't support your well-being.

If you're reluctant to voice your opinions or ask for what you deserve, ponder the following questions:

- Were you raised to be obedient and quiet?

- Were you punished or made to feel embarrassed if you spoke out as a child?

- Did you receive the information that you weren't qualified to engage in certain activities or conversations?

- Do you feel intimidated by males (or females) in power?

- How did your religion prepare you for your role in life?

- Did you see a respectful relationship between your mom and dad?

- Did your opinions count in your childhood peer groups?

- Did your opinions count in your family group?

- Why do you feel reluctant to speak your mind now?

- What thoughts or beliefs are you holding on to that reduce your ability to participate?

Are you surprised by any of your answers? Did you make some personal discoveries? If you realize that your voice has been silenced or relegated to the peanut gallery, now's the time to get your inner vocal coach on board. Strengthen your personal voice with positive self-talk and realistic counters to your cultural or childhood behavioral cues. For example:

"Yes, obedience is required to stop a three-year-old from running into traffic, and while I'm not suggesting that it's wise to compete with moving automobiles, I'm certainly capable of determining an appropriate course of action for myself. To that end, I don't need to acquiesce to everything others say out of a primal need to obey."

"Although I was raised to believe that it would be out of my league to become a scientist or the CEO of a large corporation, I know that I'm exceptionally talented in math and science, and I also have amazing people skills. I'm as qualified and driven as my male peers, and whether I want to be a scientist or run a corporation is up to me."

Nature and Nurture

Mother Nature (your genes) and how and where you were raised and nurtured both play significant roles in your overall behavior, and you actually need both influences to survive. Your DNA provided you with the foundation: your physical attributes, sex, gender, body type, and general aptitude. Then your parents, your other caregivers, and the environment you grew up in supplied the fertilizer or stimulation for your growth, along with the guidelines.

So your mother and father, who were most probably doing the best they could at the time, raised you to behave in a certain way, and your environment generally reinforced that behavior. Basically, your genes gave you brown eyes and a beautiful smile, and your folks gave you something to smile *about.* It's easy to understand why you'd feel most comfortable living within the parameters you were raised in, especially if those parameters were pleasant ones. But what if your environment wasn't so comfy?

If you were reared as I was—in a home where your mother was a stay-at-home mom who cleaned house, cooked meals, and took care of the children—you'd have a specific schema tattooed in your brain about the roles women and men play, unless your parents had the foresight to encourage you to look beyond your own backyard for inspiration. Not that those roles are in some way unworthy, but they may have been so narrowly defined that not much wiggle room has been left for you.

Reaching beyond your comfort zone requires affirmative action from you that you may not have been taught, or realized that you were capable of. News flash: regardless of what you've been told, you *are* highly capable of doing whatever you set your intention on. As you become more secure about voicing your own opinions, you'll be encouraged to participate more in the world's conversation. You'll activate your voice both on a personal and global level!

Contentment and an overall sense of well-being can be experienced when you sense that your reality is fairly represented and acknowledged; that is, when you no longer harbor a sense of discordance between the automatic responses you've been raised to accept and the way you truly feel.

As you stretch and build your new "vocal" muscles, use your environment/community as a helpmate. For example:

- ♥ Discuss your point of view with your college professor/boss/partner with confidence and self-assurance.

- ♥ Negotiate an appropriate raise in salary.

- ♥ Cultivate the ability to entertain differing opinions without losing confidence in your own.

- ♥ Raise your awareness of how external messages dictate your choices, and strive to express and validate your own opinions.

- ♥ Seek outside support from a member of the clergy, a doctor, a mental-help professional, or a life coach. Use your intuitive desire to affiliate and bond with your girlfriends. Begin by sharing your views and opinions in a forum where you know you're safe, and then branch out with confidence.

- ♥ Write down a list of your passions, your desires, your opinions on world issues, and your goals. Revisit them daily and become intimately familiar with how you feel.

- ♥ Build confidence within your circle of friends . . . and gradually test your mettle by reaching beyond it.

Take time to engage in personal introspection so that you can discover your center. Your center or core authentic self is your truth: what you believe in, what you care about, where you come from, and who you are. When you have a good sense of yourself, you're better able to view outside influences objectively as they are—merely *outside influences.*

Bear in mind that your body can't nourish itself when your system is chronically engaged in fight-or-flight mode, and neither can you project your inner sense of worth if you feel that you're continually at odds with the world around you. When you fix your own set point, define your center, and establish a narrative and sense of place that's true for you, you'll be much more able to speak up; express your opinion; and project your confident, worthy self.

Personal Tasks

♥ Make a list of your automatic thoughts or responses that are marginalizing your ability to speak your mind, such as, *I might be wrong, so I'll make a fool of myself if I speak up.*

♥ Note the cognitive distortions, such as over-generalization (viewing a single negative incident or thought as never ending), jumping to conclusions (assuming a negative outcome without definite facts to back it up), or all-or-nothing thinking (black-and-white categories with no wiggle room).

♥ Now, list the more rational responses to your initial automatic thoughts, such as, *I may be incorrect sometimes, but very often I get things right. There's no harm in stating my opinion,*

*right or wrong, because in any case both my
interlocutor and I will learn from the discussion.*

Wisdom from Your Peers

*"A woman who respects herself, trusts her instincts, loves
herself for who she is, has her own opinions, and knows
how to take care of herself is a woman with worth."*
— **Raimonda,** hairstylist, Lithuania

*"I used to think that a woman's worth came in the form
of accomplishments and hard work . . . the 'to do' list that
contained everything from grocery items and housecleaning
agendas to social events and work-related projects. I defined
my worth and the worth of others like me by the business of
my schedules and the tangible ways in which I could describe
myself to others who didn't know me. I'm a teacher, a private
swim instructor, and a mother of four. The worth I felt once
came from my titles, the things I called myself, and another
person's perception of me. Now, I believe that a woman is
worthy, not because of her titles or list of accomplishments,
but because she 'is.' Simply because she is beautifully created,
the way she is supposed to be—filled with endless potential."*
— **Heather Richter,** mother/husband's helper, California

*"Growing up, I was belittled and abused by my father, who
made sure that I knew I was nothing to anyone. I learned that*

I was worthwhile after I left the father of my two older sons and married my love, my life, my husband. He showed me who I have always been:'me.' I love myself now and my family . . . they surround me with love. I have also gained a relationship with my mom that I didn't have previously, but I lost one with my dad."
— **Brandy R. Dean,** cashier/student, California,

"I realized that women my age (55) were so prone to stereotypical expectations when we were young. Maybe it was easier. In spite of a post-high-school education, I found I still assumed that what I wanted was to find a man, marry, follow him, and have kids. I was fortunate to find a man who ruptured these stereotypes, made me think about what I really wanted, and made me realize that I didn't need anyone to 'help' me do it. My own self-worth became evident. I'm still finding out what my 'worth' means in terms of being an executive and a friend—it's all a learning curve. But it's also important to realize that our worth is relative to ourselves as well as to our many, many relationships, including those we impact without knowing it."
— **Kathy F.,** international management, New York

Journal Questions

- ♥ What steps can you take to ensure that you can express yourself with confidence?
- ♥ What's holding you back from achieving your goals?
- ♥ How is fear keeping you from moving forward?

Self-Worth Affirmations

W.O.R.T.H.
Wisdom
I am learning to communicate in multiple ways.

W.O.R.T.H.
Optimism
I am creating positive self-fulfilling prophecies.

W.O.R.T.H.
Responsibility
I am taking a proactive stance with respect to the
growth in my marriage/relationship.

W.O.R.T.H.
Tenacity
I embrace my hobbies. I create opportunities
for new experiences to flow my way.

W.O.R.T.H.
Honesty
I am willing to forgive, forget, and move on.

CHAPTER 3

Self-Esteem: Finding Your Strengths

"If we are strong, our character will speak for itself.
If we are weak, words will be of no help."
— **John F. Kennedy,** from an address he was
to deliver on November 22, 1963

The concept of self-esteem dovetails into multiple facets of you. It's connected to your sense of worth and feelings of efficacy, and it pertains to a personal evaluation of *yourself.* In an ideal world, you would hold a very high opinion of yourself, which you'd use to establish your center or set point—the rules or schema you use to navigate your life. Unfortunately, that isn't always the case, and you look outside yourself for a reflection to the people you know or the things that you do.

Come on, admit it: you care about what your mother-in-law, your neighbor, your teacher, your best friend, and even your enemies say. If people criticize you, you may deny it at first, but you'll feel wounded and very often take what they said to heart. What if after you get a new haircut, someone remarked, "Wow, you really chopped it all off, didn't you? That was brave . . . I never could have done it"?

How would you counter that? Well, if you're secure, you'd smile and accept it as a compliment for being courageous. If you're lacking esteem, on the other hand, you'd interpret the comment as a negative reflection and feel as if you made a mistake.

Now while most of us would probably assert that we were raised to believe that our inner worth is inviolate and intrinsic, when life pitches us a curveball, doubts can mess up our game and shake our resolve. For example, we may be particularly sensitive to the judgments of others and can be intimidated when other people criticize us. Some researchers even suggest that the reluctance we women feel about using our voices may stem from a deep-rooted fear of criticism.

On the face of it, criticism is merely a report from another person that points out disapproval with respect to some action, opinion, or behavior; in other words, it shouldn't be such a frightening prospect. Criticism can be constructive—a tool for learning—but for women, it often takes on a more complicated, even *sinister* significance. While criticism might indeed be delivered in full-on put-downs, it also comes in subtler forms, such as in the incessant barrage of persuasive messages females receive to be sexual, to be ultrathin, or to fit an idealized image of so-called beauty.

Criticism (or just the fear of it) can be immobilizing. You may be so uncomfortable, in fact, that you give up or give in before you begin, thus failing to compete for what you deserve. Please take the time to evaluate your behavior if you fall into this trap . . . don't let fear of criticism overwhelm your ability here, because *competition is an essential survival skill.* If you think that it's unfeminine, think again. The spoils in life aren't only provided to those who need or deserve them—you must *compete for* and *claim* them.

When you promote your best interests, you'll be improving your chances of success, and this is most certainly a survival skill worth developing. Your success upgrades not only your quality of life, but that of those closest to you, too.

Combating Negative Influences

Using negative or sarcastic criticism to persuade women to conform is a nasty but well-worn societal pastime. Our female political candidates are prime examples: they're routinely criticized for their clothing choices and hairstyles to a greater degree than their male counterparts are. Underhanded criticism causes stress and vulnerability disproportionately in the female population, and such stress has had devastating results—10 to 20 percent of young girls now suffer from some sort of mental crisis. Although stress is not solely caused by criticism, control and societal pressure on girls to conform are responsible for much of it.

Be aware of negative criticism and the intent of the messenger, and then gather strength to rise to the challenge. Remember that even though such hurtful messages are gnawing, nagging, and sometimes unwarranted; they're merely *words,* and you don't need to buy in to them. Tell the little girl inside you that she's fine the way she is and that she should set her *own* guidelines. *Remember to think for yourself.*

As a parent, I find myself using some of the same admonitions and phrases I heard in my own youth. When my folks wanted to discourage me from engaging in risky behaviors or from following the crowd just for the sake of it, for instance, they'd say, "Make up your *own* mind! If all your friends were jumping off a bridge, would you jump, too?" Of course not! And there you have it.

By the same token, one of the seminal features of cognitive behavior therapy is the stubborn refusal to buy in to an individual's sense of worthlessness. Take a look at what your internal editor says when you face criticism and pressure from others to conform, or even worse, when you berate *yourself*. Develop a new script!

If you still insist that you're not worthy, I challenge you to play a little mind game. Make a list of examples of your supposed worthlessness to try to prove it to yourself. Got the list? Now do the math. In short order you'll discover that the so-called hard evidence you present to yourself to back up your "worthless theory" will be nonsense.

The following can help you fight the negative messages you're so often exposed to and build up your self-esteem:

— Learn from criticism. If you feel that what you're hearing is constructive, heed it; if you think it's cruel, disregard it. In either case, you've learned something about the person issuing the critique. Use the lesson for motivation to excel—and then, as one of my girlfriends loves to say, "Blow it off. Put your big-girl panties on and get on with it."

— If you don't feel strong or powerful enough to confront the person criticizing you, defuse such affronts on your esteem by journaling. Release, relax, and remember that the words can only hurt you if you let them. For example, let's say that your boss gave you a negative critique in front of your peers, which made you feel worthless. Describe your feelings about the situation and get to the truth. Perhaps you'll admit, "I was pissed off and embarrassed by the critique, but the truth is that I *did* mess up on the report."

Then write down a rebuttal, such as, "I may have deserved the critique this time, but that doesn't take away from all the good responses I've gotten before. My self-worth doesn't depend upon my boss's opinion of me, and although I'm a little embarrassed, I know that all my friends still think highly of me."

Achievement and Modesty

You may think that if you're pretty enough to win a pageant or smart enough to gain access to an Ivy League college, those characteristics are what make you worthwhile. Please note that self-worth can't be built through what you *do.* Of course achievements can bring you satisfaction, but they're not entirely responsible for true happiness. Evaluating yourself solely on your accomplishments and activities is like having false bravado; it's "pseudoworth," or not the real thing. Remember to check on who you are *inside* from time to time.

The following affirmations can help with this:

- ❤ *I respect myself for who I am, not merely for what I do.*

- ❤ *I have skills and attributes, talents and passions.*

- ❤ *I have ambitions. I know that I can achieve what I set out to do.*

- ❤ *I am kind and honest, and I believe in the good in life.*

♥ *I appreciate my body and feel happy to be alive.
I treat myself well, and I pray for strength and
compassion.*

♥ *I am a worthy, valid, and worthwhile individual.*

If you're *too* modest for your own good, however, you
need to learn how to blow your own horn. Modesty and
self-restraint were preached to most of us as "good" and
"appropriate" traits to develop, and while such behavior
can be useful, be sure that you *also* develop the ability to
promote your individual accomplishments and passions.

Teamwork is an important part of life, but being part
of a team needn't discourage you from letting your unique
qualities shine. Your individual abilities and actions can be
helpful in ways the group will never know if you don't tell
them what they're missing.

And related to the fear of criticism is the worry about
being called "conceited." This is much more a "girl" thing
than a "boy" thing, but you can surely pull memories out of
your youthful past of times when peer pressure about fitting
in made you fearful of being labeled as a braggart. The
pressure to conform is a mighty powerful behavior modifier.

If you're embarrassed to tell others about the fabulous
things you've done, or you're intimidated by girlhood fears
that you'll be seen as stuck-up if you announce them,
recognize that your behavior is self-defeating, and discard
this attitude immediately. Obviously there are extreme
examples of every behavior, and excessive boasting is *not*
the goal here. Yet when you succumb to a perceived dictum
to take the backseat or play only supporting roles, you're
inadvertently denying your self-expression. Such silence

may affect your sense of worth and feelings of well-being. Using ingrained rules of modesty, reluctance, and restraint to hide your abilities isn't life enhancing; it's a recipe for disappointment.

If you have a hard time with compliments or believe that you shouldn't talk about your accomplishments, take a moment for introspection. Discern why you're hiding, as well as what you're hiding from. Come out of the closet by asking yourself soul-searching questions, such as:

- Am I afraid to tell others about my accomplishments and personal victories?
- What do I think will happen if everyone knows I'm capable?
- Do I think people will be jealous and call me conceited?
- Do I think I don't deserve praise?
- What would I do if someone told me I was too full of myself or that I was just seeking attention?
- What am I gaining from hiding my strengths?
- What will I gain from sharing them?

Build and Reinforce a Strong Character

How do you define your strengths, and how do they affect your sense of self-worth? You may automatically think of your physical distinctions, but they make up just one of your dimensions. Your inner beauty—including your mental, emotional, and behavioral characteristics—is far more telling of who you *really* are. Your *character* is your true nature, your moral fiber, the foundation from which you interact with your world. It's embedded in your concept of you as an individual, and it's the true definition of what you're worth.

When you possess a strong character, you're standing on your own two feet and relying on your faith, wisdom, and good conscience to guide your actions. The road you take may not always be the easiest to travel, but when you have a strong character, it's likely that you're going in the right direction. At any rate, you build your strongest muscles through the struggles you endure. In fact, Taoist traditions say that behind every weakness is an undiscovered strength.

The following are wonderful ways to build character:

— **Cultivate successful habits.** An incredible yoga instructor I've worked with suggests that if you do something (or, conversely, refrain from doing something) for 40 days, you can learn or unlearn a habit. It's called *willpower*—use it!

— **Develop effective social skills.** Read the paper before you go to a party, conference, or office meeting, and find two or three things that interest you as conversation starters.

— **Activate positive reflexes.** The idea here is to find the upside of any situation, so try to reframe every negative thought to see a positive aspect of it. For example, *It's raining today—I have to schlep to several meetings, and traffic will be a bear* becomes *It's raining today—although traffic will be an issue, I can take this opportunity to wear my new rain boots and listen to a book on tape, feeling blessed that the area is receiving a much-needed dose of water!*

— **Pay attention to what matters to *you.***

Dealing with Anger and Fear

Responding to life's stresses can usually be distilled down to two unresolved issues: anger and fear. These reactions are directly connected to your fight-or-flight impulses, which can be triggered when you feel threatened by criticism and peer pressure. I hate to admit it, but I have a strong anger/fear mechanism that rears its ugly head from time to time. My children have all seen it (to my utter shame), especially when they're out late and don't call. And even though I know that it's nasty, I sometimes can't keep the beast in its cage—I'll lash out at the kids when they get home even though what I *really* want to do is hug and kiss them because they're safe.

Our anger meter can ratchet up because of all manner of life stressors, including attacks on our abilities, our personalities, and our looks. While we're not running from saber-toothed tigers or woolly mammoths these days, our stresses—be they related to financial stability, career, intimate relationships, children, or balancing work with the rest of our life—can seem nearly as intense.

Increase your life span by developing coping skills now to help you tame your tigers. When you release yourself from unresolved issues of dread and rage, you reinforce your sense of worth. Belief in your *own* abilities, whatever they may be, and choosing to think positively about yourself is tantamount to a self-fulfilling prophecy. When you rise to the occasion, you'll find that you're motivated to accomplish more goals and you enjoy the process more. Very soon you'll learn that positive action motivates *more* positive action.

Recognize that the circumstances of your life have little to do with your sense of worth; rather, they come down to how you choose to think, feel, and behave about them. Acknowledging your validity as a woman is a crucial element of your growth and development, along with the expression of your self-esteem. Your innate value and validity isn't attached to the job you perform or the people you support, although those efforts may also greatly enhance your sense of well-being. Your validity is internal; you generate it yourself. Embracing your inner sense of worth requires you to *recognize* how essential you are in the full scheme of things. Once you've put yourself in a place of deserved honor, your peace with life's order will feel as natural as taking a restorative breath of fresh air.

Personal Tasks

♥   Build confidence by completing tasks you
    set out to do.

♥   Treat yourself with dignity and appreciation.

♥   Be assured that you're a highly capable individual.

♥   Let God.

♥   Express gratitude for all that you've been
    blessed with.

♥   Take a proactive action that's beneficial for
    you every day.

- Make a list of your hobbies and/or favorite activities and realize that they're your strengths and talents. Find ways to use these strengths and talents to enhance your life.

- Get off the anger/fear treadmill. Nourish your inner strength and enhance the overall quality of your life by reducing anger- and fear-related stress.

- Define daily personal goals and sustain the effort to achieve them.

- Use positive self-talk to frame your moods in a positive light.

- Expand your vision: think of five things that are interesting to you, and then make the decision to start engaging in them.

Wisdom from Your Peers

"A woman gains worth when she lives how she wishes to live: To be happy with her own choices. To have the freedom to make her own decisions. To be independent and autonomous. To be proud of her challenges and achievements—emotional and professional."
— **Elena Foster,** educator, Spain

"A woman's worth comes from self-respect; respect for others; and a confident acceptance of gender and sexuality, motherhood, and professional fulfillment."
— **Eva P.**, Austria

"I think I always knew I had worth, but I periodically forget. Adolescence is a tough time for young women— I think it's the first time we become conscious of the inequality of women in today's society. It can be unsettling and shake your foundation, but mentors, role models, and good friends can move you out of this."
— **Jessica Q.**, aid worker, Virginia

"The baby boomers helped break the ice for this upcoming generation in terms of women being valued in the world. This next generation is amazing! These girls are strong, willful, and confident. I would just encourage them to also do the interior work to build undauntable self-worth, and not let what the world thinks of their ideas and so on hinder their progress."
— **Pat B.**, executive assistant, California

"Perhaps the gravest injustice faced in the whole world is the one faced by women. For centuries we've been denied our worth, particularly the value placed on us by our families, societies, countries, and the universe. Every culture I know has its own sets of unjust views, practices, and laws toward

*women. When it comes to the value of our
worth, the global South and the North are equally
guilty in their marginalization of our issues and voice,
even if the degrees differ in its extremity.*

*"Yet, as we talk about a world that needs more peace than
wars in it, more prosperity than poverty, more health than
sickness, more happiness than sadness, and more beauty
than cruelty; humanity simply cannot attain such goals
without the full acknowledgment of women's worth, or
without the full inclusion of women in all decision-making
powers, from the family to the higher authority of the
government, of religious and of economic institutions.
Perhaps humanity's biggest act of injustice toward itself is
by denying and silencing half of its population and the
other half of its knowledge: the sacred feminine.*

*"A woman's worth is in the wisdom she brings, the strength
she has, the beauty she carries, the kindness she shows, the
courage she lives, and the patience she practices. The world
needs women so it may sustain itself. It's time to give
women the acknowledgment and recognition of their
values for justice and for a better world."*
— **Zainab Salbi;** founder and CEO,
Women for Women International; Iraq

Journal Questions

♥ What are you afraid of? Your husband? Your
father? Your teacher? Authority in general?
How can you overcome these fears?

♥ Do you let people in your life make you feel worthless? Do you give up your own power? What can you do to stop that?

♥ Do you always follow the crowd?

♥ Do you feel confident enough to take the initiative to be different? How do you express this confidence?

Self-Worth Affirmations

W.O.R.T.H.
Wisdom
I dismantle the power struggle and find my balance.

W.O.R.T.H.
Optimism
I am productive, capable, and intelligent.

W.O.R.T.H.
Responsibility
I retain my individuality. I actualize my abilities.

W.O.R.T.H.
Tenacity
I choose harmony. I find the balance in my life.

W.O.R.T.H.
Honesty
I share my feelings. I am able to build trust.

CHAPTER 4

Creativity: Living Life Artfully

"Human salvation lies in the hands of the creatively maladjusted."
— from *Strength to Love,* by **Dr. Martin Luther King, Jr.**

Do you dance? Are you a scientist? Do you sculpt, design, write, or teach? Indulging your creative impulses and engaging in activities that reinforce your inner core strengthens your sense of well-being and puts you more in touch with your authentic self. Peace with yourself and your world is especially accessible at those inspired and creative moments because it's the closest you can come to being in true harmony with the universe.

When I first entered college in 1969, I had no idea what I ultimately wanted to do with my life, and I hadn't as yet mastered a skill or found a passion that I could hold on to. But I *knew* I was creative; therefore, it seemed only natural for me to major in art. As a young coed, I made macramé bracelets and paper-flower collages—I was basically a hippie (recall the year), so much of my early artistic expression reflected that. I sewed my own clothes, knitted scarves, painted watercolors on my apartment walls, and dabbled in acrylics and oils. I also took up ceramics and got completely focused on throwing pots on my wheel, learning all about glazes, and firing up my own kiln.

Even though I eventually gravitated toward journalism, philosophy, and psychology, some form of artistic expression has remained a consistent part of my life. I've since found my passion in writing, but I continue to create in other ways as well, rarely traveling without my knitting or drawing tools. I'm thinking about taking up glassblowing or sculpture in the near future.

Have you given any thought to learning something new? I highly recommend it. Stretching your abilities, your knowledge base, and your comfort zone are highly beneficial to your overall sense of well-being *and* self-worth.

Discover Artful Living

Artful living is the ability to *responsibly* blend the necessities of survival with the aesthetics of beauty and form. Nature provides the perfect palette, since every example of design has an organic origin somewhere in the natural world—think about the infinite possibilities of snowflakes, for instance. Creativity is an encouragement to nurture your soul and take advantage of the beauty that exists in the world despite its tragedy. Your sense of aesthetic enjoyment translates to a message of vitality, hope, and fellowship for a planet that too often feels impossibly beyond your control.

If you feel as if you're a blank canvas awaiting the artist's muse (as is implied by the concept of *tabula rasa,* the theory that human beings are born with no innate or built-in mental content), I suggest that you take the position that your canvas is the foundation of a priceless piece of art. Then you can fill it with as many delightful and interesting experiences as you can.

My sister Debbie is an art teacher in Los Angeles, and she told me that she encourages students to seek vantage points *other* than the ones they've already seen. With such creative license, her pupils are energized to dream of the impossible; that is, to hope and reach for something new. Creative lessons like these can be adapted to all domains of life. The nature of creativity is that you're not restricted to one method, design, or concept—the world truly is your oyster, and *you* are the pearl!

Here are some of the things my sister has shared with her students, which I feel we should all remember:

- Acknowledge that all of the arts and sciences are treasure troves of creative experiences.

- Don't insist on perfectionism for your enjoyment; after all, the original meaning of the word *amateur* came from the Latin verb *amare,* which means "to love," and it referred to a person who loved what she was doing.

- The goal of lifelong learning and creativity isn't about earning a diploma; it's to develop a personally significant understanding of what your life experience is all about.

Let It Flow

Psychologist Mihaly Csikszentmihalyi proposed the concept of *flow*—a mental state describing what happens when a person is fully immersed in what she's doing. She becomes more *differentiated* as a result of flow experiences; she feels more capable and more skilled. Just notice how engaged your daughter is when she's working on a thousand-piece puzzle or learning to paint, along with how happy and satisfied she is when she completes her activity.

When you give your own creative impulses room for expression and focus your attention on them, your sense of well-being is amplified—your flow experience generates a feeling of energized focus and success. Whether you're skiing down a difficult run or making your child's Halloween costume, your concentration, focus, and creative involvement enforce a sense of personal control that's enormously validating. To that end, two of the many great reasons to get your kids involved in a sport they enjoy are: (1) so they learn the ability to focus intensely on an activity, and (2) to let them feel that deep sense of gratification when they're fully engaged in that activity.

Breaking out of your normal routine to learn a new skill, engage in creative activities, or to take some well-deserved downtime can improve your quality of life both physically and mentally. Studies show that women who load up their work schedules to the point that no private, restorative time is left over are more prone to high levels of stress and elevated blood pressure, which can lead to numerous chronic illnesses including heart problems. Be sure to slow down, breathe, and count to ten.

Your ability to find enjoyment in culture, nature, art, design, science, and music; and your willingness to create something new—whether it's a script, a ceramic vase, the perfect cheesecake, or an opera—engenders an aura of possibility around you that is palpable. The vibration of someone who's engaged in discovery and willing to look beyond the *tried and true* to the *brave and new* is buzzing with positivity.

I'm not trying to suggest that creative endeavors must be solitary or sedentary, however, since it might be easier for you to stimulate your muse when you connect with other people. Here are some suggestions for finding activities that you can enjoy with others:

- If you're a knitter, find a yarn shop that offers classes or group knitting sessions.
- Join a book club or creative-writing class.
- Be part of a walking, running, or biking marathon.
- Take a cooking or painting class.

Encourage Authenticity

Tuning in to your creative muse and your authentic self requires you to be self-aware, with an ability to behave in ways that are congruent with your *own* needs and moral code. Such a state of mind is called *eudemonia* and is described as a state of well-being that's obtained by living in accordance with your deeply held values.

Savoring life's many joys, appreciating the beauty of nature, and practicing living in the present helps you live holistically, thus enabling you to nurture your inner strength and build your sense of esteem and worth. Social psychologists have long studied the implications and individual differences of authenticity, suggesting that it's one of the deepest psychological needs human beings have. We all hunger for authenticity in our lives; in fact, the quest for validity is evident in all areas of life, from relationships and careers to recreation and spirituality. Our curiosity to explore and create is in part motivated by this drive.

By the way, authenticity doesn't have a specific worldly value judgment attached to it, nor is it always perfect or pretty or well organized or clever. Your authentic self is simply real—it's the *true you,* and it's the best place from which to cultivate creativity. You'll find yourself residing in such a state more frequently when you become open to experiences without censoring or distorting them. When you live fully in the moment, as can happen during flow experiences, your very self feels more fluid and malleable, open to new adventures and creative epiphanies. When you can trust your inner power source—your intuitive knowledge to guide your behavior—you may take the time to *respond* thoughtfully to life's events rather than merely *react* to them.

The ancient Sanskrit text contained within the Hindu epic Mahabharata is known as the Bhagavad Gita, and it states that you have a duty to act: to realize your full potential; to ascertain your individuality, unique gifts, and calling; and to live your life authentically. So what can you do to move into this state of being?

The simple answer to this question is this: work on building up *and restoring* your core energy. Your mind needs rest and positive stimulation just as your body does to restore your core. Enjoyable activities of all types are the breeding grounds of creative thought, so commit to an activity that allows for its expression. Be willing to investigate many areas, too, since curiosity is the foundation of genius.

Try the following:

- ♥ Spend time alone in nature—breathe fresh air, listen to all the different sounds, and allow yourself to absorb the beauty around you.

- ♥ Write in a private journal.

- ♥ Read novels.

- ♥ Visit an art gallery or museum for inspiration.

- ♥ Engage the right side of your brain by switching to your nondominant hand.

- ♥ Bake a cake, frost it, and eat a slice of it.

- ♥ Exercise—it replenishes your brain's supply of oxygen and glucose.

- ♥ Organize your closet using color coding.

- ♥ Use your willpower, since discipline is mind-altering.

- ♥ Play a musical instrument.

- ♥ Sing or write a song.

Don't imagine that you're "just not artistic." Denying your creativity is more about the *fear of failure* than an admission of inability, and allowing your fears to drive your actions not only ratchets up your stress level, it suffocates personal expression as well. Give yourself permission to create, for enjoyment is one of the by-products of performing satisfying, fulfilling actions.

Challenge Your Boundaries

Countless women have helped change the world with their creative abilities by challenging perceived boundaries. For example, Jane Austen, the talented novelist of the late 18th and early 19th centuries, used her gift with words to shed light on the imbalance of power in the male-female relationships of her day. And Marie Curie, the brilliant physicist and chemist of the late 19th and early 20th centuries, employed her creativity and curiosity to investigate the field of radioactivity. But you needn't be famous to realize that you're an exceptional human being with boundless potential; you just need to be an independent thinker. When you engage this ability, *you're exercising freedom.*

Plan International, an organization dedicated to helping children worldwide, is one of the nonprofit organizations I'm personally involved with—particularly because they sensed early on that there was a major disparity in the treatment of boys and girls. As part of their mission to ensure the improvement of all children's lives, Plan International began to research and produce a yearly report on the state of the world's girls (which you can access by going to their Website: **www.planusa.org**). Based on 2008's report, it's abundantly clear that not all females across the globe enjoy the most basic freedoms to the same degree that you and I do. Millions of girls around the world, particularly those who live in the shadow of war, are condemned to a life of poverty and inequality. So cherish your options.

Regardless of whether you have freedom to act upon your independent thoughts or not, be very clear that your ability to *have* them is virtually sacrosanct. Your thoughts are yours alone to create and manage, so use them wisely— you're creating your life with them. As Swami Muktananda said, "We create our own world by our thoughts. And thus we make our own heaven, our own hell." Similarly, Viktor Frankl, the famed Austrian neurologist and Holocaust survivor, documented his existential theory using his own experiences as a concentration-camp inmate. He discovered firsthand that his thoughts and perceptions were his alone to create . . . and as it turns out, they were the only things his captors couldn't take from him.

Keep in mind that creativity is about hope, and hope suggests possibility . . . and we all need to believe that life holds possibility. That being the case, how do *you* stimulate hope in your life? Try some of the following:

- Accumulate supportive friends.
- Live in the present and make peace with your past.
- Engage in challenging, new activities. Participate!
- Be happy with yourself—not just satisfied or making do, but truly *happy.*
- Appreciate your family members and learn the backstory; that is, your family lore.
- Be curious—make a list of at least five things you'd like to learn more about.

Religious sages point to the divine within you, and they extol you to express goodness in your actions. In the grand scheme of things, you're absolutely connected to the infinite—you're meant to excel and thrive and leave the world even more beautiful than you found it. So think of your positive actions as creations and strive to be "optimistically prolific"—because art and creativity require enthusiasm much more than discipline.

Your biggest obstacle to experiencing fulfillment in any area of your life is *inertia.* There's no limit to the goals you can attain, to the successes you can enjoy, and to the art you can create. God hasn't put a limit on these things, so why should you? When you create connections, create solutions, and create goodwill, everyone wins. In your own way, your inner artist is as profound and as passionate as Michelangelo.

Personal Tasks

- Resolve to engage in creative activities.

- Recall some of the things you used to like to do as a child (such as coloring, playing the piano, figure drawing, sculpting, gardening, or the like), and take a class that can reprise those enjoyable activities.

- Carve out time in your day for private reflection and contemplation.

- Feed your curiosity—learn something new about art, design, and music.

- Listen to classical music.

Wisdom from Your Peers

"What makes a woman worthy? A sense of purpose. A sense of self-esteem. Finding something in life that is a creative outlet. To keep evolving so that one doesn't become stagnant."
— **Diandra de Morrell Douglas,** producer, Spain

"I believe that every person is born with worth, and how you develop that varies depending on your social class or opportunities that arise. A woman's worth begins with the inner self and how she perceives herself. I don't relate worth to money when it comes to talking about a person, although many might. What you put into life, you get out of it . . . luck is possible (and timing is, too), but rolling up your sleeves and working hard to find your real worth can never be underestimated."
— **Pamela Rasey,** Ohio

"My worth as a woman comes in many forms. I feel worthwhile in the workplace, operating and performing as a powerful, professional woman. I feel equally worthwhile at

*home, cooking for my boyfriend and doing his ironing
on a Saturday afternoon. As women, we have the unique
ability to prove our worth in so many ways, from
domestic to professional to humanitarian—to enrich our
lives and those of the people around us."*
— **Alisha Rodriguez,** nonprofit/public health, California

*"I grew up in a poor neighborhood and always felt worthless
as a child. But I married a wonderful man, and we built a
business together and had four wonderful children. In all the
ordeals and trials and tribulations that we've gone through,
I think that made me realize and feel my worth."*
— **Cindy F.,** legal secretary, South Africa

*"I have never questioned my own worth.
My mother raised me to be responsible for my own
actions—as early as I can remember, I was responsible
for myself, so I had no option but to do it."*
— **Diane von Fürstenberg,** designer, Belgium

*"My parents always stressed to my brother and me that we
were worthwhile and that our value as people was tied to the
way we treated others. I always wanted to have an impact
on others, but I didn't know how to do it. For all the large-
scale volunteering projects I've done, it's the one-on-one
relationships that I've found most rewarding and that have*

*contributed the most to the way that I feel about myself.
Now that I'm a mother, I feel responsible to my children
to instill a sense of self-worth in them, as well as a sense
of obligation to those around them."*
— **Judy F.**, attorney, California

Journal Questions

* What creative urges do you acknowledge
  and act upon?

* Do you spend time creating? Do you allow
  yourself the freedom to design and explore?

* When was the last time you took a walk
  outside, alone?

* Do you view life as an optimist? If not,
  why is that? What's stopping you from
  seeing your glass as half full?

Self-Worth Affirmations

W.O.R.T.H.
Wisdom
I am creative by nature. I use all the colors in my rainbow.

W.O.R.T.H.
Optimism
My unique talents help make the world a better place.

W.O.R.T.H.
Responsibility
I acknowledge my creative abilities.
I am proactive in using them.

W.O.R.T.H.
Tenacity
I seek answers. I am willing to explore the world
around me and take my blinders off.

W.O.R.T.H.
Honesty
I am willing to discover what thrills and fulfills me.

PART II

Relating: Taking Responsibility for Your Worth

"When I was told 40 years ago that I should learn to type so I could someday type papers for my boyfriend, I didn't know what I wanted, but I knew it wasn't that. It's an act of hubris to think that things can be truly different, but hubris was what I had—hubris, and the millions of other women who knew that there must be more to life than waxy buildup and a frost-free freezer."
— **Anna Quindlen,** journalist and author,
from a piece written for *Newsweek*

"I think that I've always known I had worth, but life has its challenges, so we must be kind to ourselves and others. If we make spiritual deposits in our soul, then when times are challenging, we'll have enough self-worth to carry on with grace."
— **Jo Ann Ralston,** Oregon

"A woman's worth can be found in the working world or at home. Either way, it's determined by a sense of purposefulness. Everyone—men and women—needs to feel that they have a purpose on this earth. For me, creating a home and raising children has given me a sense of purpose and worth. While the success of my children and my husband are due in part to luck, genetics, and their hard work, I do believe that the background support I've provided has played a part. And for me, being in the background has been a comfortable place to be. Worthiness can come from the network of friends a woman develops and the experiences that are shared. The warmth and comfort of the home a woman creates can also be a measure of worthiness."
— **Leah Fischer;** mother, wife, attorney; California

CHAPTER 5

Assert Yourself: Taking Charge of Your Narrative

*"Experience is a hard teacher because she gives
the test first, the lesson afterward."*
— **Vernon Law,** baseball player

Are you comfortable acknowledging and expressing your own personal power? What does that mean, anyway? *Power* can sound like an aggressive word, so you may feel awkward using it in a sentence that describes you. Try to look at it in a different context: imagine that personal power is your inner driver or the engine that generates forward, confident movement. Even if your engine is in silent running mode, it's still producing energy.

Unfortunately, you may have been taught, or learned experientially, to keep your power hidden. These questions will help you discover if that's indeed what happened to you:

● Do you avoid stating your opinion in front of male colleagues?

● Do you feel insecure about your abilities and knowledge base?

- Were you raised to think that women were the weaker sex or that they couldn't compete with men in sports, business, and finances?

- Can you rise above and beyond a societal stereotype that consistently views you as basically shy, obedient, and emotional?

Whether it was articulated or left unspoken, you prob-ably grew up surrounded by the attitude that there are certain frailties associated with being female, and it can be a tough one to shake off. Your personal power, meaning your unique inner currency, is wrapped up in your feelings of worth—and too often you either doubt its existence or just give it all away.

How have you coped with societal dictates that have the power to silence or marginalize you? Can you ignore them now? If you were raised to believe that masculinity equals strength and intelligence and that women must demur to a man's opinions or wishes, it can be very intimidating to challenge that belief. Are you confident enough to debate misguided preconceptions?

Hopefully, you are. Still, your responses to life's situations can be so programmed by enmeshed cultural and societal influences that they become automatic. You may not realize you're doing it, but in many subtle ways, you give up power all the time.

Think about the following:

- Do you have an equal say in the division of labor in your home?

- Do you handle your own finances?

- Is your career viewed as being as important as your spouse's?

- Do you have control over your own time and body?

- Do you assume supportive roles without acknowledging their true value?

- Have you become a "shadow personality" or a wallflower?

- Do you follow along or act compliant rather than stand up for what you believe?

- Are you confident enough about your opinions to voice them freely?

- Do you find that you often need to give up or give in?

- Do you form your own political opinions; or do you feel pressured to align yourself with your partner, husband, father, or other figure of authority in your life?

You must face the challenge and assert yourself. When you activate your personal power, you step up to your full potential.

Learn to Be Flexible and Resilient

Assessing yourself (including your abilities, goals, and attributes) and then *asserting* yourself is confidence-building behavior. It also builds *resiliency,* which is defined as "the ability to cope and adapt to difficult and/or challenging situations." Even as you grapple with a unique set of challenges every day, all of humanity is faced with a changing world that requires almost constant adaptation. We're all obligated to become more proficient at what we do: to work harder and longer, to deal with trauma, to cope with setbacks, and to overcome adversities. And while we're born with the capacity to develop resilience, it's not a skill we're typically taught.

Resilient people can power through difficulties, and they can survive and thrive in tough situations without acting out in dysfunctional ways. Those who are resilient—think supple, pliant, flexible, and elastic—more easily recover from traumatic experiences.

The ability to be flexible not only results in your being a better, happier, stronger, or wiser individual, it could also very well ensure your survival. So take affirmative action! Here are some tips for doing so:

— **Take charge of your mind and body.** Learn to manage and stabilize your emotions, health, and sense of well-being by reducing stress, exercising, eating properly, and getting an adequate amount of sleep. Walk, talk, eat reasonably, and laugh—these are simple instructions, but they're amazingly effective.

— **Seek to solve problems in a *productive* manner.** When you focus on the problem rather than the emotion dredged up by it, you'll be using what psychologists call problem-focused coping. This skill helps you build resiliency muscles.

— **Foster a strong inner self and be proud of who you are.** This is known as a "positive self-concept," and it can be strengthened and tuned by simple interventions such as repeating affirmations or upbeat self-talk.

— **Develop the ability to convert misfortune into fortune.** The old adage, "If God shuts a door, somewhere He opens a window," comes into play here, as does the concept of serendipity. Life is full of changes, turns in the road, and challenges—all of which can be seen as opportunities. Make a conscious choice to view them that way.

Overcoming the Need for Conformity and Helplessness

Out of exhaustion from fighting the zeitgeist, you may on occasion be tempted to give in to get what you want, rather than show strength and risk being ostracized, condemned, or ridiculed.

It's important to note that the reason our ancient ancestors didn't challenge the status quo came from a very tangible fear of being left out of the tribe; that is, conformity was expected and necessary for survival. Following this mind-set along evolutionary stages into the more recent Puritan era, female obedience was considered vital for community building. Many of our current cultural mores and stigmas reflect these old developmental guidelines, and we're subconsciously adhering to remnants of antiquated rules.

Regardless of how strong your primal instincts may be, those evolutionary neural road maps needn't dictate all of your current behaviors—you *can* form new habits. Since your safety often depends upon your ability to use your mind, mental strength and stamina are actually survival skills. And when you have knowledge, you have access to power; it's a simple concept. *Education is key.* This is why one of the first and most important goals for the women in war-torn Afghanistan and Iraq was to reestablish schools for girls. In this way, the 50-odd percent of the population that had been kept essentially powerless would have the chance to eventually effect positive change in their societies.

Your potency lies in your ability to use what you've learned to make your life (and the lives of those around you) better. The following can help:

— **Reevaluate your automatic responses.** Is your urge to conform instinctive or truly relevant to your current situation?

— **Remember that being part of a collective requires give-and-take behavior,** even for an individualist. Are you comfortable with the concessions you make to fit in, or do you harbor resentments? Do be sure to assert yourself and share your concerns.

— **Learn to respect your own wisdom and developmental path.** Conformance needn't necessarily be ego shattering. Making compromises is an integral part of life, yet bear in mind that such behavior is *still* a choice.

Understand that assuming a dependent, submissive role doesn't build up self-esteem; it encourages a feeling of helplessness, and that is *not* what we want. *Learned helplessness*—a psychological principle that describes what happens when an animal or person has come to believe that she's helpless in a given situation, even if she has the ability to overcome it—is a debilitating condition that, unfortunately, many women languish in. This state can arise from a perceived lack of control over life, which can mess mightily with the individual's sense of worth, validity, and raison d'être.

I remember how helpless I felt when I was in my early 20s and was struggling to combine motherhood with an outside source of income. Although I was trying to take care of my little ones, I knew that I needed to earn money of my own . . . yet I was constantly in a tug-of-war with the major wage earner of the family about my duties and my ability to affect the family budget. My participation in the management of the family income in those "Wild West" days of my life was limited because my contribution wasn't deemed significant. And for a long stretch of my life I believed that nonsense and felt extremely vulnerable.

You can avoid such a fate by asserting yourself. Start small if you must—but take a step forward. Here are some suggestions to get you started:

- Learn a new skill.

- Discuss your *equality* with your mate before you set up house.

- Speak up at meetings.

- ♥ Advocate for something you care about.

- ♥ Vote—this is another way to use your voice.

- ♥ Give of your time, talent, or treasure to help someone who's disadvantaged.

- ♥ Start your retirement fund.

- ♥ Challenge yourself. Take responsibility for some task that you thought you weren't capable of handling.

When you unlearn your helplessness, you'll achieve a more equitable distribution of power between you and the men and other women in your life. This may seem like one of the hardest bridges to cross, but do it anyway because it's an important threshold. Assume your right to exist, and *value your own participation* no matter where you happen to be on the food chain. You'll build upon your strengths by honestly assessing what they are.

You Can Be Confident and Proactive

When you can invoke that feeling of self-assurance that comes from an honest evaluation of your abilities, you'll exude confidence—the strength of knowing that you're capable. When you're positive that you can change things or impact situations, you're significantly more likely to succeed.

As the Taoist scholar Deng Ming-dao said, "No matter how extreme a situation is, it will change." When you're confident, you're also much better able to *handle* change when it comes. When you know who you are and can acknowledge the woman within, you'll be better prepared to equalize your playing field in whatever game you engage in. Ultimately, the rules you play by will be much more fair and balanced when you have a higher stake in establishing them.

Even though asserting your intellectual prowess may appear to be at odds with the mind-set that women were put on the planet to be used as helpmates rather than leaders, don't let that stop you . . . just as you mustn't allow antiquated stereotypes to challenge your very being because of the number of your chromosomes.

We've had numerous defiant, proactive, and assertive female forebears who have shown us another way to function. One of the most valuable lessons we can learn from these mentors is that they took initiative. When *we* take the initiative, we project the message that we're willing *and able* to move forward in the driver's seat. Yet why is this concept so difficult for many of us?

Ask yourself now what stands in your way of achievement. It's entirely probable that your answer is fear, albeit a deep-seated one, such as:

- Fear of failure
- Fear of abandonment
- Fear of ridicule
- Fear of criticism

Percolating beneath the surface of your actions might be the fear that if you disclose how much you *really* know, you risk rubbing competitive males the wrong way, which spelled disaster in our ancient past. You may unwittingly avoid exhibiting your smarts because of that pesky little prehistoric brain map called "survival instinct."

However, in the *current* millennium, be aware that your fear of being assertive is misguided and maladaptive. Current studies show that in order for women to get ahead in business, they usually need to be *more* assertive than men. Remember that your instincts are in place to keep you alive—since they're meant to warn you about danger, be on high alert. It's dangerous to be reluctant to act or to be insecure about your abilities. If you're indifferent about your life's course, you're going to endanger your overall sense of well-being and quality of life. Be more afraid of *that.*

You weren't meant to be a shadow person who lurks in the background or stands patiently (and perpetually) on the sidelines. Be inspired by the gains your female ancestors achieved. Armed with such stellar motivation, challenge yourself to make the changes you seek in your own life. Even though you're genetically wired to be *process oriented* rather than *solution oriented,* focus on the result you wish to attain and then use your process-oriented instincts to map out the best route to get you there.

Try the following:

- Take an active role in your family's financial planning.

- If you're not comfortable with your financial acumen, make an effort to learn how to balance your budget and prepare for your future.

- Stay abreast of political happenings and global news. Form educated opinions and be willing to discuss and debate them.

When you're assertive, your presence is essential. By *presence,* I'm referring to your ability to maintain self-awareness. When you exercise this ability, your personal power (that is, your personal *intention*) is on duty. Please note that having presence and exuding your personal power has very little to do with being king of the hill, because clearly you're not always going to be the leader. *Life is about teamwork.* It's just fine to have a supporting role; what's crucial is that you feel *validated* and are *valued* for it. Realize that your sense of power and worth gestates inside of *you.* Yes, your employer might be in charge, but you need to feel that you're engaged in a fair relationship and that your responsibilities are an important, valid, and valuable part of the whole.

Personal Tasks

In your journal, make a list of the things you can do to be more assertive. What I've listed here are examples—you should contemplate what's currently going on in your own life and then hone in on the actions you personally need to take.

Here are some ideas of what to write (always state your assertions in the present tense):

- *I find my voice. It is a huge leap, but I have to learn to articulate my opinions.*

- *I use my voice to express gratitude for what I have and who I am.*

- *I find the courage to step forward and take a leadership role at work, at school, at home, in clubs, or at my place of worship.*

- *While I may have chosen a supporting role in life, I acknowledge that my contributions are vital and valid. I set my own standards of excellence and rise to them.*

- *I imagine future goals, both for myself and the world at large, feeling optimistic as I do so.*

- *I acknowledge that my own actions have an impact on my life; I intend to act positively.*

- *I take ownership of my personal currency and activate my personal power by acknowledging my innate value and worth.*

- *I use positive affirmations to help me express my worth—I know it's been proven that an optimistic outlook can shift my mind-set and set me up for a much more positive, productive life.*

- *I work on forming new habits that promote my sense of well-being.*

- *I stand up for myself by acknowledging my validity.*

♥   *I take responsibility for my own ability to make
a difference in my sense of well-being, and I
decide to be happy. I remind myself that only
I can create the life I live.*

Wisdom from Your Peers

*"I think that what makes a woman feel worthy is a sense
of herself. It's so easy to lose that in the trappings of what's
popularly seen as womanhood. There are expectations,
now more than ever, for a woman to 'have it all': a family,
a successful career, intelligence, cunning, beauty, and
sensitivity. No one would ever expect so much of a man.
So I think it's easy for a woman to get lost in that, trying
to balance all of the aspects of her life with all of the
expectations of her. She may have the career, but she still
needs the marriage (or vice versa), then once she has that,
there's always the obsession to make it better, stronger, or
more successful (however, I think that this is the American
way). I think a woman truly finds her own worth by
looking inside and doing what it is that satisfies her, not by
succumbing to the pressure of what is expected of her."*
— **Tina Tyrell,** photographer, New York

*"I was a fat kid and largely a social pariah as a child, so
I've had to work at realizing my own worth. I discovered that
you can increase your worth. My advice is to treat
everyone as though they have worth; giving someone
their dignity is never a mistake."*
— **Kat M.,** USA

"What defines a woman's worth? I think you are what
<u>you think</u> you're worth. It's your self-esteem and love of self.
Some women are beaten and believe that they're supposed
to live that kind of life. I believe that women complete men
and vice versa. You just need to find your soul mate."
— **Cindy F.**, legal secretary, South Africa

"When asked the question of what makes a woman worthy,
I immediately reflect on my life being raised by my mother.
I experienced her as a powerful human being, so being female
in no way stopped me from thinking that anything was
possible. My mother stood for equality, and I witnessed her
sharing the responsibilities 50-50 with my father. Therefore,
if a woman feels that she's doing her part to contribute
to something or somebody outside of herself to make a
difference, then she deserves the feeling of being worthy."
— **Lili Gross;** designer, mother; California

"Women are the foundation of families. Men are icing on
the cake—and the icing can be very important."
— **Tricia Dressler,** producer, Georgia

"My two daughters were born deaf. Everyone in my family became depressed and desperate, and I had the courage to stand up for my children, smile, and make sure they got to live a normal life. I succeeded by taking them to a 'normal' school every day. I found orthophonists to teach them how to read books and read lips. I wanted my girls to live as happily as all the other kids, and they got used to wearing hearing aids. With a lot of work, they learned to speak French fluently along with English!

"My 27-year-old daughter received a cochlear implant in 2007. I knew that I'd cry when she heard my voice for the first time. I've always been there for my kids. We love each other, and that makes life worth living. This is how I experience my own worth."
— **Daniele Matalon,** artist, France

Journal Questions

- How can you become more assertive in your life?

- Do you feel resilient? Do you bounce back from life's difficulties? If not, what would make you feel more secure and confident?

- Do you surround yourself with people who are supportive of your goals and ambitions? If not, why is that?

Self-Worth Affirmations

W.O.R.T.H.
Wisdom
I know that independent thinking is a form of strength.

W.O.R.T.H.
Optimism
I have innate abilities and unlimited potential.

W.O.R.T.H.
Responsibility
I take a holistic view of life. I am multifaceted.

W.O.R.T.H.
Tenacity
I believe in myself. I am continuing to grow.

W.O.R.T.H.
Honesty
I remember that confidence in my abilities builds
self-esteem and inner strength.

CHAPTER 6

Sex, Love, and Intimacy: Understanding and Enjoying Your Sexuality

"I used to be Snow White, but I drifted."
— **Mae West**

Regardless of what our mothers taught us, when we came of age and sex hormones flooded our brains, we started to yearn for that forbidden, seductive, carnal knowledge. As a species, our sex drive is a survival instinct. We need to reproduce; it's in our DNA. But for us women, our sex drive is obviously more than an instinctual need; it's wrapped up in feelings of comfort, love, companionship, excitement, naughtiness, and hope.

Your desire for exciting, satisfying sex is totally healthy—and you were prompted all of your young life to believe that it's on its way via a constant onslaught of media messages. Some of those messages began when you were a little girl in the form of fairy tales. You probably enjoyed all of those stories about the handsome prince who inevitably swooped in on his magnificent white stallion to carry a fair maiden in distress off to his castle, where they lived happily ever after. Yet what began as a nebulous childhood desire would eventually mix with age-appropriate female hormones and turn into a deep and intense longing.

It's entirely normal to want an emotional and intimate relationship with another person, and on some level you're aware that your happiness will be heightened once you've had satisfying sex. And you know what? You're right. Learn to trust your instincts.

A healthy sex life is not only enjoyable; it's an integral part of your overall feeling of wellness. Studies show that:

- Having an orgasm triggers the release of the feel-good chemical *oxytocin,* which makes you feel more trusting, relaxed, and energized

- Sex stimulates your immune system—regular sex actually makes you less vulnerable to colds and the flu

- Prolonged deep kissing can lower blood pressure, and it releases bacteria that stimulate the production of antibodies

- Sex can be a great cardio workout that also improves overall circulation and flexibility

Religious and Societal Views

Your instincts for sex are so strong that it requires great mental and physical restraint and/or religious commitment to deny this urge. So unless you've chosen a nonsexual life, your own sense of harmony will be best achieved when satisfying sex is a part of it. If you haven't made peace with your early sexual indoctrination by now, it's time to bring negative attitudes to the surface and revise them.

Edit the inappropriate or self-diminishing rules out of your current belief system, and start to put a positive spin on your outlook of sex. Even among the most faithful, sexual expression within a marriage blessed by God is honored. So make peace with your religious beliefs. Your positive outlook will strengthen your overall sense of self-worth and make your sexual experiences more fulfilling.

Try the following:

- In your journal, write down some thoughts about how sex fits into your relationship. How does your perception differ from your partner's?

- If you feel guilty about having sex, examine why you feel this way. Come up with statements that counter your guilty thoughts with a more positive view.

- Seek a healthy outlook about your body, your sexual appetite, and your mental health.

- Make it your business to learn how your body functions and what makes you feel good.

- Meet with your trusted spiritual counselor to gain insight about how sexual activities are meant to fit into a healthy relationship according to your religious doctrine.

Sex is thrilling when two people are *equal* participants. But take care, because a lot of societal messages strongly—and wrongly—define women as sexual objects.

The need to control female sexual activity has prompted some men to dominate women by using fear and force. In your ancient past, you actually would have preferred to be dominated by a man rather than be abandoned by him, but such instincts were for survival. In the here-and-now, you most assuredly wouldn't want to allow that instinct to guide your actions.

You're less likely to be subjected to domination when you're secure about your sexuality and claim rightful ownership of your own body and its functions. You may be the object of someone's *desire,* but you're not an object yourself. If you're not experiencing a positive sexual relationship, or if you feel dominated or abused, something is wrong and you need to take steps to make changes. Here are some suggestions to help you do so:

- ♥ Know that while society sends plenty of messages to you about what you should do to become more sexy and appealing, along with how you should perform, you only need to listen to what feels right *for you.*

- ♥ Discuss your sexual relationship with your partner—*outside* of the bedroom, in a non-threatening environment. Be as honest and open about your feelings as you can.

- ♥ Seek counseling from a professional who specializes in sexual relationships.

- ♥ If you're in an abusive relationship, seek immed-iate help from authorities. Emergency resources are available, so use them. Muster up your true survival instincts, and *get the hell out of Dodge!*

The Joy of Sex

Profound, trusting relationships with other people form the foundation of your personal community; your network of family, friends, and business associates is essentially your universe. Such positive, mutually beneficial connections can intensify your sense of self-worth. Your one-on-one relationships are so important to your existence that you may even set your personal compass by them. If you're a mother or part of a couple, you have a very specific sense of what I'm talking about. I am the mother of four, the grandmother of four (okay, I started young), and married to a man whom I adore—my world virtually revolves around all of them. I'm sure that many of you would agree that your lives are similar in that your relationships rule.

Still, your one-on-one *sexual* relationship will take trust and intimacy issues to a different and perhaps even more vulnerable level. As with nearly everything else in life, you must have a personal stake in the enjoyment of this relationship and be proactive about your participation in order to wield any personal power or control over it. And I'm not talking merely about aggression and surrender here. *Dancing in the dark* to a tune that seduces you both requires some skill, so acquire an intimate knowledge of your own body and your partner's. Be willing to learn new sexual techniques, suspend your embarrassment or fear of vulnerability, and *allow* yourself to trust. Trust, as you've surely discovered by now, is an important component in satisfying sex.

While you may feel reluctant to talk about your pleasure zones, to pinpoint your feel-good places or positions, or to discover where your G-spot is, try to conquer your fear—because a big part of developing trust and intimacy with someone else is learning to dismantle some of your *own* self-imposed barriers. Discovering what makes you feel good and knowing how to pleasure yourself opens you up to new experiences. Although I know that my husband prefers to be present when my pleasure bell rings, for instance, the fact that I know how to ring it by myself is actually a turn-on for him. *Do* try this exercise at home, and then share the results with your lover.

When you assert yourself sexually, you'll discover parts of your personality that you never knew existed, and the sensations you awaken will not only be appealing and seductive to your partner, they'll be empowering for you as well. The benefits for you will be, in a word, *orgasmic.*

Here's how to make this happen:

- **Choose to have sex**—make it a priority in your relationship.

- **Find a birth-control method that works for you, and practice "safe" sex.** This means that you need to be aware of, and guard against, sexually transmitted diseases.

- **Practice what makes you feel good!** Research shows that women who masturbate and have *mastered* their own turn-ons are eager to have sex with their partners more often.

- **Be willing to talk about what pleases you** and ask about your partner's pleasure zones. Fantasies are great, since your mind is part of your sexual experience, too—a very *big* part.

- **Be honest about your experience**—you don't need to fake an orgasm. Sharing your true feelings builds trust and intimacy.

Speaking of *orgasm,* the word is defined as the height of sexual excitement, characterized by feelings of pleasure centered in the genitals. I'll bet your discovery of the climax is one of your most salient memories . . . and it's an event you re-create often. Good for you—that is, if you've *actually experienced one.*

It turns out that national surveys of adult sexual behavior state that 75 percent of men report always having orgasms, while only 29 percent of women say they do. As noted earlier in the chapter, researchers tell us that satisfying sex is an important additive to our overall well-being, and our ability to enjoy gratification in this area is obviously as important for us as it is for men. Did you get that? Repeat after me: "My sexual satisfaction is as important as my partner's. It's okay for me to admit that I need and enjoy it."

While sex should be healthy and fun, as well as contribute to your overall sense of well-being, your gratification (or lack thereof) doesn't get much societal airplay; the media doesn't advertise ways for women to reach *their* "peak." Hmm, I wonder why. There are numerous drugs on the market that promise to keep penises hard, and TV commercials and print ads have turned Viagra into a not-so-secret weapon that all but guarantees performance.

In addition, it seems that if a man has erectile dysfunction, doctors consider it an emergency. But if *you* can't reach a climax, do you rush to the emergency room? I didn't think so. This seems to be because, despite years of investigation into the female orgasm—including the famous "Kinsey reports" of the early 1950s—confusion about it persists.

Perhaps evolution and Mother Nature played an unfair trick on us, in terms of the survival of our species, since female orgasm serves no adaptive purpose. We don't need to have an orgasm to get pregnant, and as many of us report, the penetrating act that's generally required to deposit semen in the procreative conception zone isn't as successful at producing orgasms as nonprocreative acts such as masturbation and oral sex. Go figure.

The fact is, female orgasm is complicated, mysterious, and not a guaranteed by-product of sex. Yet when you experience one, you'll think you've discovered nirvana. As at least 29 percent of you know, it feels *really* good. Confusion about them notwithstanding, orgasms are definitely worth having, and you owe it to yourself to discover your best method of achieving them. By the way, self-discovery and masturbation are not the makings of witch's brew; it's *your* body and you have a right to see how it works . . . and enjoy the process, too.

Love and Intimacy

Romantic intimacy, that most sacred of emotional states, is something most of us desire and in fact need. The motivation to fulfill our needs is potent, and it apparently follows a specific order. Just as there is a time for all seasons, our species' development evolves according to recognized stages.

Psychologist Abraham Maslow came up with the concept of a "hierarchy of needs." This theory posits that once physiological and safety needs are fulfilled, human beings want to meet our social needs—that is, to be loved and to belong. Interestingly, sex actually appears as a primary need in Maslow's list; however, sexual *intimacy* doesn't appear until the third position in the hierarchy, along with family and friendship.

Here's a brief rundown of the hierarchy, which moves from the most basic human requirements to the more complex:

1. **Physiological needs**—breathing, food, water, sex, sleep, homeostasis, and excretion

2. **Safety needs**—security of the body, employment, resources, morality, the family, health, and property

3. **Love/belonging needs**—friendship, family, and sexual intimacy

4. **Esteem needs**—self-worth, confidence, achievement, respect *of* others, and respect *by* others

5. **Self-actualization needs**—morality, creativity, spontaneity, problem solving, lack of prejudice, and acceptance of facts

I'm sure you'd like to think that love is the most important thing in your life. However, as you can see from Maslow's hierarchy, sex—the primal instinct to mate, to procreate, to satisfy that hot and lusty urge—comes first on the list of needs. And while it's clearly also very important, sexual intimacy seems to have less pull. It's *third* on the list, at least in Mr. Maslow's evaluation, and therefore will be satisfied only after your physiological and safety needs are met. Do you agree with this hierarchy? I sometimes wonder.

As a young girl, I was forbidden to act on my sex drive—I was told it was wrong to succumb to those urges until a ring was on my finger and a religious ceremony was performed. I sublimated the power of my sex drive into a desire for romantic love. My love and belonging needs became my wishes and dreams, but they were inextricably linked to my sexual desires. While it may be true that sex is one of the primal physiological needs that must be met before one can advance to the next level, in my cultural upbringing, love *or something like it* was supposed to come first.

Regardless of drives, urges, and hierarchies, few would argue with the fact that love is a crucial part of our lives, connected as it is to our sense of well-being and worth. Love makes the world go 'round;' some say it's what makes life worth living. Many will seek love through sex, but as you know, sex doesn't automatically lead to love, and love doesn't guarantee that you'll have great sex. The romantic fairy tales of your youth notwithstanding, the blend of love and sex requires commitment, a special type of chemistry between you and your partner, and an ability to build intimacy.

That right chemistry that combines love with sexual intimacy is an intoxicating brew, one that you thirst for. Your personal pharmacy of brain chemicals goes into action when you engage in intimate behaviors: studies show that just a 20-second hug starts the flow of oxytocin. Often called the "hormone of love" and the "cuddle chemical," oxytocin (yes, the same one that's released during orgasm) is one of the feel-good chemicals that instruct you to relax, enjoy, let down your defenses, and trust.

When you have a trusting relationship, you feel safe, calm, and remarkably free. You can experience a sense of liberation when you can be honest about your feelings—for it is there within your intimate connections that you can share your deepest, most profound thoughts without fear of reprisal. Such relationships are definitely worth having.

Creating a Safe Space

Sexual intimacy obviously requires a great deal of trust, as you literally bare your body and often your soul to another human being—no defenses, all is exposed. Such intimacy is a combination of your animalistic drive and the cerebral bonding experience you yearn for.

In other words, intimate revelations aren't limited to discussing what turns you on. Getting to the heart of your feelings and sharing what you believe to be true and valuable is closer to the point. Your private disclosures deal with some significant truths about you and provide a forum for airing your opinions, judgments, and complaints. In a protected space that *you* create, you can rag on other people or bitch about your boss without feeling compromised. You should also:

- Be willing to unveil your secrets and bare your soul
- Trust your partner
- Encourage honesty and curiosity

Secrets come in all shapes and sizes, with different complexities and inherent energy. Some of your intimate secrets will be cries for help (that is, you feel sad, physically or mentally wounded, or scared) and others will simply help you vent disappointment (such as when your best friend gets a promotion instead of you and you feel like a failure). Regardless of the content, intimate, trusting, and revealing communications with someone you care about are highly important for you.

That said, sharing your deepest, darkest secrets isn't easy—it takes courage and the promise of confidentiality. Although it's possible to fall in love at first sight, true intimacy is built in stages. To sustain a connection, you need to be able to trust each other. *Trust* is the operative word here: unless you trust that you're safe and secure, your intimate interactions will disappoint; you'll fear that your admissions will be ridiculed, misunderstood, or judged.

To successfully build intimate, trust-filled relationships, you'll want to consider bringing the following to the table:

♥ A safe environment for sharing; that is, a safe harbor

♥ An awareness of your mental filters—use restraint and resist the urge to critique and edit the information you receive

♥ Effective communication skills, including listening—when you listen attentively and *unconditionally* to your partner without interrupting with suggestions, solutions, or commentary, you open the door to a very safe space

- ♥ Unconditional, positive regard

- ♥ Honesty

- ♥ Fidelity (duh!)

- ♥ The permission to have differing opinions

- ♥ The ability to lower and suspend your defenses

- ♥ Confidence

- ♥ Empathy

- ♥ Assertiveness and the opposite of that coin— vulnerability

Believe it or not, the trust you need for building intimacy can best be forged when you feel good about *being you.* Your experiential wisdom—the result of learning from your experiences and adapting those lessons to your life—is an essential element in the creation of a more content, confident, and accessible you. Your strong, positive sense of self will then be secure enough to allow another person in to your private places. This combination of characteristics in a one-on-one relationship is sublime, empowering, and soul enhancing; and it contributes to your sense of well-being and worth.

How to Attract Love

If you haven't found your love yet, perhaps you need to stop looking *out* for it and start looking *inward* instead. I'm sure you've heard this advice numerous times, but if you aren't heeding it, you're going to stay stuck in place, floundering and repeating past mistakes ad infinitum. Think about your life circumstances right now. Are you sabotaging your chances for intimacy because of feelings of guilt, inadequacy, or shame? Do you claim to be too busy to dedicate time and effort to building an intimate, loving relationship? Are you reluctant to be honest, show your vulnerability, and reach out to someone? Are you so afraid of failure that rather than attract someone to your life, your attitude rebuffs a potential partner? Are you sticking to an idealized, set image of what a person must do to love or be loved by you?

Your own distorted expectations of what a perfect match should be may be building walls around you that are insurmountable. The chances of finding true love grow exponentially if you have the right attitude about it, and that attitude includes *loving yourself.* Try enjoying every part of you: your physical attributes, whatever they are; your mind; and your abilities. Do some role-playing—pretend you're in love and wrap your arms around that feeling. Resist the negative, self-doubting thoughts that pop into your head and take yourself out to dinner. Decide to enjoy *your* life, and then set out to do so.

Focus on the following:

- Self-respect
- Realistic expectations

- ♥ Positive personal regard
- ♥ Self-worth
- ♥ Conscientiousness
- ♥ The ability to adapt
- ♥ Self-assurance
- ♥ Self-reliance
- ♥ Personal power

When you absorb the fact that you can't force love to come in to your life, you realize that you shouldn't be in angst over it, and you begin to relax. You'll instantly become more attractive when you do, and your attractiveness will be palpable to others. There's even a law of nature that describes this phenomenon: the Law of Attraction. This has been documented and written about since the early 1900s and states that there is a physiological foundation for positive thinking. Based on the reality that there are many forms of energy and energy cannot be destroyed, the law suggests that you essentially attract to your life whatever you give your attention, energy, and focus to, be it positive or negative.

The Law of Attraction states that you can purposefully project specific vibrations to prepare yourself for love and ultimately bring it your way. So try vibrating these four things:

1. An aura of affection
2. Optimism
3. Openness
4. Positive intention

When these four elements collide, all manner of doors will open for you, including the one that has love on the other side. The alchemy created when you come from a positive, self-loving place is far better than any fairy-tale ending could ever be. Miracles do happen; and if you open the right doors (and windows), then, as the saying goes, love *will* find a way.

Setting the Stage for Longevity

It may be wise to add a few notes here about what *not* to do in relationships. A couple of the biggest no-no's are power trips and jealousy, which are anathema to satisfying relationships. Why? Because an inequitable distribution of power in a relationship can shrivel your attempts at intimacy. Jealousy has to do with possession, territory, and greed—not love. Not only is jealousy an expression of anger and distrust, it's also deflective and damaging behavior that chips away at your self-worth. Don't go there.

Let's face it: love doesn't grow in an environment that has been constricted or constrained. There will always be outside influences and extraneous stimulation that could inspire, delight, and distract you or your lover and cause you both to look in other directions. Jealous chains can't hold your partner's heart any more than they can hold yours. While chains (such as the ones provided by possessiveness, control, anger, and an abuse of power) may temporarily confine the body, the mind cannot be tethered and can fly wherever it wants to go.

In the end, there will be times when your lovers leave and love doesn't last . . . that's life. There are simply no guarantees that close relationships will endure. Your chance for longevity will depend upon your ability to defuse power struggles and to grow in the same direction. Seek connection while retaining your individuality, and normalize your playing field by maintaining harmony. Although there is no perfect balance of power in your busy, complicated life, you can find ways to do the power shuffle in an even-handed, *harmonious* way.

It's also important to make an effort in your relationship and beware of complacency. Once you think that every door has been opened, you might stop opening doors. Set the stage for longevity and strong bonding by building a solid foundation and working to keep your romance alive.

Being romantic suggests an idyll, or the fantasy of the unexpected. The pleasure of romance is the kick of discovery, the agitation of curiosity. Every touch is a breakthrough; every conversation is virgin territory. Be willing to reinvent your relationship by keeping that "new-discovery spark" alive.

Naturally the blush will eventually leave the rose, but you don't want to neglect your garden altogether. Continue to express a twinkling sense of novelty to your lover at surprising and unusual times. Leave the ubiquitous communication devices on silent (or put them away altogether), and focus on devoting time and attention to *each other*. Trust me—the return on your investment is worth it.

The following are wonderful ways to keep your spark alive:

- Look at your mate through interested eyes.
- Say the words *I love you* every day.
- Be kind.
- Give compliments and encouragement to each other.
- Share feelings and fantasies.

- ♥ Be willing to be vulnerable.
- ♥ Learn acceptance and adaptation.
- ♥ Be open and honest.
- ♥ Trust each other.
- ♥ Build a solid, positive sense of self, yet be willing to be selfless at times.
- ♥ Develop good communication skills, including— and perhaps especially—active listening.
- ♥ Be charitable. Learn to give.
- ♥ Take turns. Share.

And even though lovers often tell each other, "You complete me," the truth is that you need to be thoroughly complete in your own right. The two of you comprise an entirely new entity—a relationship—and each of you is *100 percent* responsible for your "couple system's" success. Your ability to share your multidimensional self with another human being is one of the most compelling and organic features of a satisfying relationship. When your sense of self-esteem is positive and your personal power light is turned on, you'll continue to grow as a person in tandem with your development as a couple.

Love is worth giving *and* worth receiving. It's so important in your life that you'll spend a great deal of time thinking about it; desiring it; and, hopefully, living it. Thus, treat it like your garden and nurture it every day.

Love is playful, positive, and hopeful. Love has a sense of humor. Love grows in all sorts of different, imaginative, and creative ways. Every bit of energy and positive attention that you devote to it will pay dividends; love is the currency the universe thrives on. Make deposits into your love account daily.

Personal Tasks

- Learn to compromise.

- Acquire and build your ability to be assertive.

- Disagree without demonizing. You and your partner are *both* individuals, so you both have a right to your opinions.

- Recognize that very often when you make concessions or compromise, you're not *caving* in, you're *staying* in.

- Think *compassion,* not *competition.* Chill out. Revisit hot issues when you've cooled off and can reopen the door of reason.

- Resist the urge to push each other's buttons (you know what I mean!). Button pushing is a no-win, inflammatory activity.

- Retain individuality—remember that who you are inside is what your partner fell in love with in the first place.

- Self-esteem—build it, feel it, nurture it.

- Let love grow. Tend to it and protect it, because it is precious.

Wisdom from Your Peers

*"A woman is worthy when she defines herself and her life
by her values, her morals, and her devotion to the family unit.
Then when she sees herself through a loved one's eyes,
she sees someone who believes in herself."*
— **Florence S.,** entrepreneur, Malaysia

*"Men in our culture too often grow up thinking of women
as somehow lesser. Both daughters and sons should be
taught the truth: that women are not only a civilizing
influence on men, but full and equal partners in life, and
that men and women together can create a whole that's
greater than the sum of its parts. Women's gifts may
be different from men's, but they're no less valuable,
and any male who fails to understand this risks losing
out on much of what's best in life."*
— **Carrie Kelley,** personal shopper/gift specialist,
Massachusetts

*"I've been very lucky in my life to be graced with
natural intelligence and an outgoing personality, along
with parents who raised me as an equal to my brothers.
When I think of women's worth, I think globally, to the
dismal situations for women around the world who are
deemed worthless: female infanticide, FGM (female
genital mutilation), 'honor' killings, and so forth."*
— **Nancy C.,** pharmaceutical quality advisor, Vermont

"I lived in a wonderful neighborhood for three years; I had my third and fourth children while I was there. My life was full of change—I had four small children depending on me and a husband who traveled frequently. During my time there, the women in this neighborhood served me. They brought me meals, helped with my children, talked with me, made playdates at the park, and laughed with me. They gave themselves to me at a time when I had nothing to give. For the first time in my life, I felt worthy. I felt valued. I felt unconditional love. As others served me, they could not have known that what they were giving me would last a lifetime.

"How could their thoughtfulness heal my wounds? How could their service teach me that I am a valuable person? I was humbled and thankful. My eyes were opened. I could do nothing in return for my neighborhood friends, but that didn't matter to them. They loved and cared for me regardless of what they received in return. What an incredible lesson I learned about worth! Could you imagine what our world would look like if we saw the needs of others? If we reached out—not at a time that's convenient for us but when there was a need. What if we saw all people as worthy? Wow . . . we would live in paradise!"
— **Heather Richter,** mother/husband's helper, California

Journal Questions

- Do you enjoy sex?

- What do you like most about your relationship?

- What steps can you take today to make your love/sex life more enjoyable for you and your partner?

- Do you have a reciprocal relationship? Do you feel that your intimacy needs are being met? If not, what can you do to change that?

Self-Worth Affirmations

W.O.R.T.H.
Wisdom
I stay "me" in all my relationships.

W.O.R.T.H.
Optimism
I am capable of having lasting love.

W.O.R.T.H.
Responsibility
I reconnect with God in my own special way.

W.O.R.T.H.
Tenacity
I keep my passions alive!

W.O.R.T.H.
Honesty
I take myself on an adventure and acknowledge
that I matter . . . because I do.

CHAPTER 7

Marriage: Making It Work for You

*"My advice to you is to get married. If you find a good wife,
you'll be happy; if not, you'll become a philosopher."*
— Socrates

Are you among the approximately 57 percent of U.S. women who are currently married? If so, how's it working for you? Aside from the obvious aspiration of setting up house with the person you were hot for, why did you decide to wed—especially since the divorce rate continues to vacillate somewhere between 40 and 50 percent? How does your marriage affect your self-esteem? Are you like the many women who say that they measure their sense of worth and value by the success of their marriages?

It's clear that our people connections are important to us; our tribal instincts are strong. But why do we need a legal, binding agreement to keep us in line? Can't we just "live together without the tether" if we're so inclined? (Lots of us actually do: in 2005, the U.S. Census Bureau noted that one in ten couples they surveyed was unmarried.)

It turns out that our preconceived notions and expectations about marriage are filtered through whatever cultural mores we've grown up with, and those schemas can be strong motivation for our behaviors. In broad strokes, marriage is considered an institution and, as such, is frequently thought of as a recognized and anticipated stage in life. A recent survey of young college women found that no matter what career course they were pursuing, most *assumed* that they'd get married and have children one day.

Religion may be a key motivator here. Whether you happen to be religious or not, there's no denying that faith has played a big part in societal expectations about marriage. In fact, the beginnings of the male-female marriage unit can be found in the Bible. Eve's curiosity about the tree of knowledge and her subsequent bite from the forbidden apple resulted in God casting both Adam and Eve out of Eden—He condemned the two first biblically documented humans to a life of labor, tilling the ground from which they were created. God then decreed that Eve's desire was to be for her husband, Adam, who was to "rule over" her. Eve's punishment was even more severe, for she was ordered to bear the agony of childbirth.

Even as cultures have evolved over time, they've continued to transmit signals and claims about marriage that haven't necessarily had women's best interests at heart. Female virginity was (and continues to be) valued in many cultures, and it's traditionally been associated with our worth.

Let's take a look at the term *bride-price.* You see, back in the day, a woman's value as a wife was calculated by the men in both her family and the groom's family; and once agreed upon, it was paid to her father! The bride's virginity was a necessary element, since without it, she could be considered worthless and unfit for marriage.

The question of virginity and the possession of a woman's supposed value could be notoriously harmful to women in ancient times—in some cases, it even resulted in death. Yet some of these culturally enmeshed and murderous practices persist today in so-called honor killings. This oxymoron describes the horrific torture and death inflicted upon women who were found to be unchaste: they were seen to have dishonored their families (particularly the men) by having sex prior to, or outside of, marriage; or by being immodest in their dress and/or behavior. Such murders are an artifact of the past that are somehow resistant to global pressure to desist. Although they're universally condemned, honor killings are still carried out in some countries . . . to their utter *dishonor.*

These are mind-numbing realities. While humans are variously thought to have more or less appeared on the scene some 40,000 years ago, the basics of marriage haven't really changed all that much. Stereotypes about what men and women are supposed to do in a marriage, as well as who's supposed to be "in charge" of whom, have been passed down to us through the ages.

At the risk of sounding totally unromantic, wedlock seems to have evolved out of a very basic societal need: to sustain monogamous units long enough for us to procreate and nurture our offspring to self-sufficient survival status. Marital bonds are society's way of ensuring that we don't wake up every morning on the hunt—with an urgent need to seek companionship, sexual partners, and potential fathers for our children.

Marriage has always had an aspect of community building; but it's also traditionally been concerned with territory, property, ownership, male honor, and the continuation of a man's family bloodline.

One of the rituals that is a part of many marriage ceremonies is the "giving away" of the bride from the father to the groom. Another custom that suggests ownership and property can be found in the giving and taking of the husband's last name. Women in many cultures, including my own, drop their own family surname when they marry to assume another identity as Mrs. So-and-So—the adjunct of their Mr.

Like many of you, I followed this cultural prescription. You'll notice that the name I've used on the front cover of this book is Cheryl *Saban,* not Cheryl *Flor.* I thought about the whole "name game" when I married, and I made a conscious choice to take my husband's surname, which I'm proud to do. However, I'm also aware that this is an example of how some of our cultural rituals and customs are so embedded that it can feel unnatural, uncomfortable, or even disagreeable to change or denounce them.

If you're conflicted about changing your name, be honest about your feelings and decide on what makes you feel good. Regardless of whether you take a new name, retain your own, or hyphenate the two, the most important take-away message here is to maintain your identity and your sense of self . . . and you can do *that* no matter what name you go by.

Do You Have a Healthy, Harmonious Union?

If you're married, ask yourself what your union means to you. Do you consider it your rock, the foundation upon which you build your life? Is it the framework for all of the activities in your life: a companionship, an economic enterprise, a sexual outlet, the admittance to a tribe, a support system, a friendship, and a parenting dyad? If so, you're not alone. For most of us, marriage is a serious commitment to blend two sets of childhood rules, family groups, varying opinions, unique perspectives, and different behavioral road maps into one new, functional, long-term unit.

For those of us who marry, there are multiple motivations for walking down the aisle, including:

* Love
* Financial security
* Children
* Monogamous sex
* Religious beliefs that forbid sex until marriage (in other words, to have sex, you must wed)
* Long-term companionship
* Perceived obligation or duty as a female

Many women state that they gain enormous pride, self-esteem, value, and a sense of worth from their successful marriages. That would make sense, considering that marriage is actually *good* for their health. Studies suggest that married women are 30 percent more likely to rate their health as excellent compared to single women, and wives are five times less likely than single or divorced women to be victims of crime.

Since marriage makes a third of us feel healthier and safer, does the experience also make us happier? The determination of how marriage affects *the quality* of our life depends, in some part, on the time and culture we were born into, as well as the religious guidelines and social mores our parents, tribe, and/or community raised us to believe in. But there's another element that comes into play here: our personal intentions.

Marriage, like any partnership, necessitates effort from you. You'll need to be able to negotiate to get your needs met, learn when to make compromises, and recognize when to stand your ground. Marriage is not always easy, and it has its own growing pains. Know that actions speak louder than words—if you're looking for enduring happiness, you need to walk the walk. In other words, act like responsible adults who love, respect, and admire each other.

Creating a pleasurable marital environment requires you to seek *harmony,* not *hegemony* . . . what a concept. Harmony can seem like a quixotic quest in your hectic life, but keep going for it. Your self-esteem and sense of worth are important components in any successful relationship, but they're particularly vital for your marriage.

There will be plenty of give-and-take. And though you may need to do some negotiating about the roles you take on in your union, the development of a happy partnership depends less on the roles you play than your willingness or desire to play them.

Here are some helpful hints:

- Understand the roles you play in your marriage.
- Be willing to learn how to keep your marriage intact.
- Strive to maintain harmony; be willing to entertain a different perspective.
- Maintain your individuality, but seek togetherness and intimacy.

Dealing with Divorce

If marriage enhances your sense of worth, does ending your union diminish it? If you've ever gone through a divorce, you'd probably answer the above question in the affirmative—at least during the initial aftermath—because the experience can be so hellish. You'll require some new coping skills, a different way of looking at society's rules, and the passing of time in order to live through the toxic fallout of a divorce. Self-esteem can take a nosedive. Self-worth? It can feel as though it was never there. Those of you who have gone through it know that at its most benign, divorce turns your life upside down; at its worst, you feel discarded, outcast, and worthless.

I'm in my third marriage—and have been happily, blissfully wed now for 22 years. I'm so joyful and content, in fact, that I can reflect on my *other* marital experiences and share the truth about them without breaking out in hives. Nevertheless, disturbing recollections of my past are still crystal clear.

Since we've all been socialized to use marriage to define ourselves, when it fails, we may take it personally. I certainly did. Divorce didn't fit into my hopes and dreams for a happy life: it was viewed negatively by my family and my religion; it symbolized failure. Now it was bad enough that I got divorced from my *first* husband, but when my *second* marriage ended as well, I wanted to hide under a rock. I watched helplessly as my whole world changed—my friends, my location, my rituals, my social networks . . . everything. It was discouraging to say the least; *devastating* would be a better descriptor. And it wasn't this way just for me; the emotional backwash of the experience nearly undid my two daughters from that first marriage as well. Now in their 30s, these two precious girls are still grappling with psychic wounds that the experience of *my* divorces inflicted on them.

All these years later, I'm the mother of four (I had two more children with my third husband), and I consider myself a three-time married and successful woman. Yet even though I believe that I've made amends for my mistakes and redeemed myself, as it were, I can *still* dredge up suppressed guilt and feelings of inadequacy about my life choices. Three times married makes me a two-time loser in some minds, and this is a powerfully negative concept. Such traumatic change can wreak havoc with a person's emotions *and* health, and I have firsthand proof of this: the sadness, anxiety, and feelings of failure nearly sent me into a tailspin. I thank God; my lucky stars; and, okay, my own actions for pulling me out of it.

A broken heart, shattered dreams, and a feeling of time lost can all weigh heavily on your mind and consequently mess with your high-level thinking processes. Even when two people choose to be respectful and cordial to one another in divorce, the impact on their lives may be similar to the death of a loved one. Divorce is, at least temporarily, a marginalizing and traumatic experience, so it's best to try to avoid it. Yeah, right . . . this is easy to say, difficult to do.

Letting Go of the Past and Moving On

I sometimes wish that I could see into the future, but it's not one of the skills I've been able to develop. However, my hindsight *is* 20/20: I know that even though I paid a high price for them, I learned some lessons. I'm of the opinion that all of our experiences are valid and ultimately teach us something. That said, *it is our responsibility to learn those lessons.*

Be the director and producer of your life, and design an existence that's fulfilling for you. While you can't predict the future, there are steps you can take to tip the scale of marital happiness *and* life success in your favor. For example:

- Set up a lifestyle that promotes growth; that is, keep learning.
- Communicate your feelings.
- Seek compatibility in religious beliefs and parenting styles.
- Grow roots, as well as wings; remember that love is not a possession.
- Show compassion and empathy.
- Be willing to open doors to new experiences.
- Retain the freedom to build on your own inner strengths.
- Be a visionary who imagines that your relationship is strong and fulfilling.
- Know that enjoyable experiences you work for have lasting power.
- Build your life on a positive foundation of trust.
- Strive to be happy.

The unpleasant truth is that even with all the best intentions, people (including the ones you love) make mistakes, so learn to forgive. If the problem isn't worth getting divorced over, you just need to forgive and forget and get over it. Who wants to drag around emotional baggage like indignation, hurt, and anger? It feels awful—

giving you stress, gray hair, and frown lines before your time—and nobody wins. It may be difficult to imagine getting over terribly hurt feelings, and there certainly may be times when wounds are too deep for a mere "I'm sorry" to heal the pain. But holding on to bitterness and anger is incredibly damaging to you.

In many cases, you can shift your feelings in the direction of forgiveness by simply deciding that you're going to make that shift. And keep in mind that forgiving someone doesn't mean you're agreeing to support actions that are inappropriate and wrong. Forgiving is as much about healing *yourself* as it is about the other person. It allows you to move on.

Forgiving, accepting, acknowledging, and negotiating are all important aspects of a long-term relationship; but in an *intimate* relationship, there are additional components. One of the most important of these is passion—when you work to keep it alive, your marriage has a much better chance at longevity.

Behave Like Lovers

While *passion* does refer to sexual excitation, it's also about the zeal and ardor you have for something, as well as the devotion (or intention) you have for it. Keeping your passion alive first and foremost requires your *intention to do so*. There's an old saying that goes something like "If you don't use it, you lose it," and studies suggest that there's some truth to that.

Don't allow your passion flame to sputter—be it your sexual passion or intense devotion to your hobbies, sports, or career. But in particular, pay attention to your marriage, since this is *not* a dress rehearsal. If you love your spouse and want your union to survive, be proactive. Try the following to stoke your passions:

- **Improve your intimacy skills and be willing to take adventures.** There are books for this—use them. Psychologists call it "bibliotherapy."

- **Get your "sexy" on.** Change your pattern and move beyond your standard routine. Try putting on a blindfold, closing *or* opening your eyes, putting on something sexy or taking every-thing off!

- **Hug each other**—a long, warm, sensuous, sincere embrace that allows you to feel your partner's heartbeat. Just 20 seconds will start your brain producing feel-good chemicals such as oxytocin to help get you in the mood.

- **Feel embarrassed, timid, and titillated again** by using toys, lotions, and seductive clothes and movements. Sex and erotica are *not* just for frisky teenagers and hot-to-trot young lovers.

- **Pretend that you just met** or it's your first time for sex, and everything is new. Then remember you're *not* a novice—shift your sexual drive into first gear by putting into practice what you already know.

- **Be willing to engage in new activities and hobbies of any kind.**

Marriage *can* be a joyful, compassionate partnership. Those who are successful at it learn to make room to grow, and they cultivate the capacity to let things flow. Aside from the obvious commitment to love and to honor each other, most happily married couples are *kind* to one another. Here are some tips you might use to bring more sweetness and joy to your own relationship:

- Act the part of love.
- Trust and be trustworthy.
- Share spiritual beliefs.
- Admire each other.
- Be flexible and sensitive.
- Follow through on your commitments.
- Be conscientious—be responsible.
- Let go of rigid rules.
- Touch each other emotionally and physically.
- Be affectionate in small ways daily.
- Use positive words, deeds, and intentions.
- Create a pleasurable environment.
- Treat each other kindly.
- Learn to forgive.

Remember the seminal message of the '60s? It was: "Think positive." While positive thoughts alone may not be able to change a situation, a positive attitude *can* spur you to a similar action. To frame it in psychological terms, positive thinking is a coping skill—it's a form of psychological resilience and a characteristic we could all use more of, particularly in our marriages. Think positively that you'll be part of the 50 percent of marriages that succeed, and really love the one you're with.

Personal Tasks

- Pursue goals for your marriage that are harmonious and within reach.

- Maintain financial independence.

- Continue to grow as a person—learn, be curious, and build independent muscles. Keep in mind that excessive dependence on others can make you depressed, and it certainly won't encourage satisfaction and fulfillment, be it individually or within the context of your marriage.

- Practice forgiveness.

- Stay physically and mentally fit—take care of your body and keep opening your mind.

- Vary your activities—as the saying goes, variety adds spice to your life.

- Observe your religion and pray—seven out of every ten Americans report that they do so every day, and they're able to build positive emotions because of it.

- Practice optimism and take pleasure in the joys of life—hard-won pleasures are the lasting ones.

Wisdom from Your Peers

"What makes a woman worthy? Good values, self-respect, loving her family, loving her friends, giving to the community, and taking care of herself mentally and physically."
— **Vicky M. Taipei,** restaurateur,
People's Republic of China

"Regarding what makes a woman worthy, I can't speak for other women, but only for myself: for me, worth is the appreciation of loved ones, especially of my husband."
— **Ulrike D. Frankfurt,**
mother and home manager, Germany

"Because of what I do for a living and the social and political activism that has made up a large part of my life, I'm sometimes lauded by others. I suppose that moments like those, such as the night I won my Oscar, would be viewed by people outside my life as being when I felt worthy. I do feel honored and grateful for those moments. But the moments that truly make me feel worthy are much smaller and probably have much more in common with women around the world than the glamorous moments.

"I feel worthy when one of my children has a victory. I feel worthy when someone tells me, as they often do, how unspoiled and kind my children are. I feel worthy when I can make my 84-year-old mother have a deep-belly laugh. I feel

worthy when I teach a class of students about the profession that I cherish. I feel worthy when I stare down my fears and stand on a stage in front of an audience. I feel worthy every time I try something that I've told myself I can't do, like sing, paint, or swim on a swim team! I feel worthy that I am able, for the most part, to cop to my many mistakes and make atoning for them a part of my life. I feel worthy that I asked the world to send me a soul mate and that my prayers were answered when I met my husband."

— **Mary Steenburgen;** actor, wife, mother; Arkansas

"I'm lucky in that I feel I know and respect myself, primarily on account of the drive and motivation that propel me forward. I'm very curious, a people-to-people person, and I feel comfortable in my managerial position. I'm convinced that the key to shaping my persona was the excellent upbringing I received at home and the energy imparted by the cosmos. There's no doubt that this energy is renewed and reinforced when, at the end of the day, I come back to the warmth of my nest, the support of my husband, and the love of my children."

— **Yona Bartal,** assistant to president Shimon Peres, Israel

Journal Questions

- ♥ Do you feel fulfilled in your marriage?
- ♥ If you've gone through a divorce, have you fully recovered your sense of self-worth?
- ♥ Do you harbor feelings of failure in your marriage?

- What can you do to recharge the passion of your relationship?
- How can you continue to grow as a person?

Self-Worth Affirmations

W.O.R.T.H.
Wisdom
I start to express my self-worth now. I know that my life is not a dress rehearsal.

W.O.R.T.H.
Optimism
I cultivate happiness in myself, and I inspire it in others.

W.O.R.T.H.
Responsibility
I get to know myself and appreciate who I am.

W.O.R.T.H.
Tenacity
I seek help when I need it.

W.O.R.T.H.
Honesty
I avoid dysfunctional, angry, or otherwise negative thoughts and behaviors.

CHAPTER 8

Motherhood: Defining the Role of a Lifetime

*"Mothers are fonder than fathers of their children because
they are more certain they are their own."*
— **Aristotle**

As a child of the '50s, I was raised with visions of Betty Crocker, the iconic "perfect woman" of that day, dancing in my head. Many of us from that era were habitually exposed to illustrations of pretty housewives in shirtwaist dresses and delicate organza aprons just like Betty, who served up beautifully decorated cakes and pies while their beaming children stood nearby. Part of our education process, these images projected the type of woman we were supposed to emulate. Such a female—who was adept at all of the finer points of cooking, cleaning, housekeeping, and child rearing—was held up as the standard for young girls in my culture. She represented what we should reach for, how we should look, and how we were to behave in order to be valued in society.

Every woman I remember seeing in magazine ads (or on the few television shows I had a chance to watch in my younger years) was a mother. Even today, marriage and motherhood provide the subtext within which girls are encouraged to organize their place in life. For many females, these two dominant roles not only provide the subtext of self-worth, but they're also the very foundation of it.

The basic conceptualization of mothering is a theme that reaches across cultures; a common language women everywhere can speak. That's not to say, however, that all of us are *fluent* in it. Contrary to well-worn stereotypes, our domestic roles aren't necessarily ordained by human nature, biology, or men's and women's psychology; they're the result of overlapping factors including historical circumstances, race, religion, time period, and social practices. And it's not a foregone conclusion that *all* women will become (or even desire to become) mothers, nor does it assure that once we become mothers, we'll be able to do the job well. With that said, motherhood continues to be a defining role that many of us crave.

Being a mother can mean different things to different wo-men, including:

- ♥ The burden and/or benefit of added responsibility
- ♥ The end of innocence
- ♥ Independence from the parental home
- ♥ The beginning of adulthood
- ♥ A woman's "duty" or destiny
- ♥ Fulfillment—as in feeling fulfilled as a person
- ♥ Faith in humankind
- ♥ The desire to nurture and love
- ♥ Legacy—the continuation of a bloodline
- ♥ Selfless love that's deep and enduring

A Mother's Worth

Are you a mother? If so, you're among friends: there are an estimated 82 million moms in the United States alone. If you think that your relevance as a woman is wrapped around your ability as a mother—if it gives you a sense of self-worth, value, and validity—accept major kudos. Take responsibility for the value you add to your kids' lives, for, as they say, children are our future. Always keep in mind that your strength, ability, and input as a mother/teacher/nurturer to your offspring are valid and necessary components in the way the future of society unfolds.

In other words, take your power seriously.

Becoming a mother is a whole-body experience that requires tremendous endurance and courage because giving birth is neither easy nor painless, no matter what the books say. Of course adoptive mothers won't escape running the gauntlet; they'll go through emotional labor pains, too. However, those of us who have experienced a vaginal birth know all too well the pain associated with it, regardless of the fact that the words most commonly used by Westernized medical professionals to describe labor include *uncomfortable, strong, contractions,* and the like.

Phooey. A stone in your shoe is uncomfortable—giving birth is *hard,* and in many cases, *really* painful. What women go through to eject a child from that inner sanctum of a womb seems superhuman, even surreal. If you ever have a chance to witness it firsthand, I highly recommend it because you'll never take birth for granted again. Trust me—every time it works, it's a miracle. The act of giving birth still claims the lives of 500,000 women each year.

When you become a mother, it can seem entirely natural to define yourself based on your status. You take on all sorts of monikers: "soccer mom," "alpha mom," "stay-at-home mom," "working mom," or even "empty-nester mom." The challenge of motherhood can tax you more than other functions or roles you take on, but I'm sure you'd agree with many parents who say that the payoff is greater, too. And one significant gain is the sense of capability and inner strength derived from having a substantial and positive impact on the life of another human being.

Motherhood is a work in progress—a project that has a beginning but no clear ending. No matter what else you're doing, pursuing, and accomplishing in your life, you can be sure that being a mom will be your central focus. The rituals, customs, and social constructs that determine how your own experience will play out depend upon your own cultural upbringing and the environment you live in.

Yet in many ways the birth and mothering process is the same for us all: it generally requires a lifetime of strength, patience, and compassion to be done successfully. Does it affect our sense of worth? Hell, yes.

It Takes a Village

Do you think that society treats you fairly because you're a mother; or do you sometimes feel that you must work harder, longer, and with less compensation for the services you provide? You may never entertain such questions—most women who responded to my questionnaire about worth stated that motherhood was hands down one of the most important and fulfilling areas of their lives. Who cares if they have to work harder and longer and receive little or no positive feedback? Many of the respondents stated that they're so devoted to their children that they'd protect them with their lives, if need be.

Some women find their strength in mothering and report that the tools they needed just came naturally. These tools include:

- Patience
- Endurance
- A proficiency at multitasking
- Courage
- Selflessness
- The capability to stand up to the things that go bump in the night
- Faith
- The ability to work 24/7, even while sleep deprived

For some women, these tools *do* come naturally, but not for all. Just look at the shelves of any bookstore and you'll see entire sections devoted to motherhood, parenting, child rearing, and so forth—we obviously still have plenty of questions. For something that's supposed to be intuitive and natural, there does seem to be a lot of room for confusion.

The subject of motherhood commands plenty of media attention: we hear about it on Oprah Winfrey's show, and we read about it in women's magazines. Women also participate in mommy-and-me groups, mothering circles, and other support communities to discuss parenting issues and to discover better ways of tackling the life-altering business of raising a child.

Many women know this secret: when they devote every asset of themselves to others—be it to a partner, parent, friend, or child—they can get lost along the way. You can avoid this fate by developing yourself in parallel to your little ones. Your ability and desire to start new activities and to grow as an individual will help you keep your unwieldy emotions in check when your kids individuate away from you. Continue to grow, and redefine who you are.

In addition, look into establishing a network of support with other women through the aforementioned groups or by assembling a "girlfriend posse": with more than 82 million mothers in the U.S. alone, you should be able to connect with a few of them! Support is crucial when you're raising children . . . it really *does* take a village.

Here are some especially helpful tips for mothers:

♥ Stay engaged with other family members and friends—especially your girlfriends.

♥ Remain interested in the world around you. Try something new.

♥ Take a vacation with your spouse, with friends, or both.

♥ Join a group or club that allows you to participate in a sport or activity that takes place outside of your home, preferably in the great outdoors. Nature is the best healer.

♥ Communicate, share, and laugh about your experiences with others. Even crying with other

women can smooth out the ragged edges of
your nerves when you hit particularly rough
patches of motherhood.

♥ Keep your primary relationship (the one with your
spouse or partner) on track. As overwhelming, all
consuming, and exhausting as parenting can be,
you need to keep your couple connection strong.

♥ Plan dates to have one-on-one adult time.

♥ Don't lose your sense of humor.

Family Planning

Family planning traditionally refers to birth-control
methods, but it's much more than that. It's critically
important to actually *plan* for the welfare of your family . . .
especially when you realize that raising children requires
funding. So can you truly support another human being?
Are you prepared for the level of attention you'll need to
give—the selfless devotion that's required?

A family plan will need to address the mother's career
and whether or not she'll go back to work after she has
children. Most women do. Studies show that approximately
63 percent of moms in the U.S. return to a career outside
the home after childbirth. But even though the majority
of mothers return to work, the transition from postpartum
parents back to career women can be difficult. Leaving their
infants in the care of others can dredge up conflicts, resentments, and complicated emotions; however, once they get

beyond their initial reservations, most women are content with their choice. Many moms are happier when they get back to work, in fact, finding that they're getting the best of both worlds. Children who are watched over by compassionate caregivers in positive environments fare well, too.

Although studies show that mothers are still unfairly passed over for high-level corporate advancement, we're a resilient and resourceful bunch. Many among us have found alternative pathways to vocational fulfillment and financial stability via online businesses and part-time or flexible work schedules.

If you're trying to find alternatives to the traditional nine-to-five career platform, try the following:

- ♥ Seek career counseling. Such professionals may have ideas for you that you've never thought of.

- ♥ If you have an entrepreneurial spirit, consider starting an online business. Check out eBay for examples of what other women have done.

- ♥ Talk to your company about the possibility of working split shifts and using flextime.

- ♥ Work from home. With current technology trends, your ability to "stay in the loop" will only get better. Thanks to cell phones, laptops, and wireless-Internet devices, you can now conduct business from anywhere in the world.

- ♥ Seek help from peers and mentors. Determine options that allow you to grow professionally, without jeopardizing your ability to function as a full-time mom.

In the past, female duties traditionally centered on the home and children; there was no shortage of tasks that needed to be performed to keep the home fires burning. Today, even though most women work outside of the home, they still tend to take on the role of organizing the care and well-being of their children. They also typically worry more about how they're going to pay for their kids' needs than men do. A recent study of couples in America found that 63 percent of women were stressed out about money compared to 51 percent of men.

Financial sustainability and security is a valid worry; after all, the ability to maintain your livelihood and that of your children is a critical component in successful mothering. Regardless of your spouse's input, motherhood requires a *huge* commitment on your part. So are you able to provide for your family financially? Whether or not you're bringing in a salary in addition to managing your home and parental duties, you need to be financially savvy.

Again, family planning comes in handy here. Try the following:

— **Be honest about your finances.** Can you afford to raise a child on your own? If not, does your spouse earn enough to do so? What adjustments can you make to ensure that you have fiscal independence?

— **Seek financial advice** (with your spouse or without), and then create a budget that protects both you and your children. If you find yourself alone due to divorce or death, you need to know how you'll survive. *Make a plan.*

— **Set up a savings/educational account for your child at birth.** Keep in mind that kids have a tougher time leaving the nest these days and you'll be a mom forever. Think ahead about your children's higher-education costs, as well as how you'll guide them to independent living.

— **Make an agreement to be given a sum of money** that is *yours alone,* particularly if you're a stay-at-home mom relying on the financial input of your spouse for survival. Call it your salary and feel good about it, because you deserve it. And be sure to save a portion of it for a rainy day.

De-Stress and Stay Healthy

Part of being a good mother is managing your own health. I hope that you're paying attention to it, since your ability to function at full capacity as a mother may be jeopardized if it's at risk. Your health problems could put your kids at risk as well.

As you may have already discovered, women are more susceptible to stress-related disorders. Postpartum depression (a form of depression that many new mothers face), for instance, is a serious condition that requires knowledgeable, professional attention. Learn how to recognize emotional pitfalls, and then develop coping skills to mitigate them. When you notice your fuse getting short, stop, feel, and listen to yourself.

Take a moment to consider these questions:

— Are you tired, frustrated, and cranky?

— Are you angry and/or sad? Do you lash out at your spouse and/or children?

— Are you wound too tight? Note that too much stress can lead to chronic fatigue syndrome, fibromyalgia, back pain, headaches, depression, and so on. Seek help if you think that motherhood is stressing you out.

— Are you sleep deprived? Most mothers are, but note that sleep deprivation can lead to more severe problems. If you're not sleeping (because your kids aren't sleeping), try the following:

- Cut out caffeine, tobacco, and alcohol.
- Don't take your work to bed with you.
- Vary your schedule so you can take catnaps.
- Meditate.
- Practice calming visualizations and body-relaxation techniques when you go to bed.
- Learn new coping skills.

Understand the highs and lows of your emotions, along with how you handle situations. Without proper coping skills, your body may pump you full of too much cortisol and adrenaline—chemicals that can wreak havoc with your equilibrium. Emotions pack a strong punch, and you can count on their working overtime when you're a mother.

These de-stressing coping skills can greatly help you smooth out your emotional responses:

— **Breathe, meditate, and take a time-out.** If you stop, count to 10 or 20 (or whatever it takes for you), and breathe in and out deeply and slowly, you'll actually feel your body calm down. It's a fact—I've personally used this technique as an intervention on numerous occasions.

— **Read up on parenting and be prepared.** Prevent your emotions from running away with your calm, logical self by preparing yourself in advance. There will be difficult times, but remember that what you *do* know is less intimidating than what you *don't* know.

— **Know yourself.** Self-knowledge is key to understanding what emotional land mines you should avoid. Strategize and set up personal boundaries to protect yourself from wandering into them.

— **Exercise regularly.** Oh, I know that you think you don't have time. But if you don't exercise your body regularly, your health will be jeopardized. Clearly, if you're using all the bulbs in your chandelier, you'll want to take precautions so that doesn't happen. At the very least, take a brisk walk: you need 10,000 steps per day to keep your body functioning at optimal levels.

— **Good nutrition is vital, so eat a balanced diet.** (Duh.) This includes consuming vegetables, whole grains, fruit, and protein. Forget about processed foods—eat the *real* meal.

Your children need you to be vital and mentally and physically healthy, and *you* need yourself to be that way as well. So if you're struggling with health issues—and that includes both physical- *and* mental-health issues—don't put them on the back burner. Treat yourself as if you're as important and worthwhile as everyone else in your family, and reach out for help.

A Role for Life

When does a mother's job end? Never. Once a mother, always a mother. (Of course it's the same with fathers.) So what happens when your kids grow up, move away, and plunk you into the famous empty-nest stage? How will this transition affect you? Well, for one thing, you'll have a lot more time on your hands. Having said that, your mind will probably still spend plenty of time dwelling on, and worrying about, your adult children, so it's wise to be prepared for this transition before it happens. You don't want to be like some women, who feel utterly lost and sad when their kids grow up and move away from home. When their offspring leave the family nest to begin lives of their own, these ladies have a tough time picking up the scattered pieces of their own identities. They've put their needs aside for so long that they forget what their needs truly are.

I'm currently going through the "launch" phase of my youngest daughter—she's my last little bird to take flight, and even though I knew in advance what to expect from the previous three children-cum-adults to leave our nest, I was still very sad. I tried to keep my tears to a minimum, and I did mostly shed them in private, but I nevertheless went through a process of mourning the loss of a little girl who used to climb into bed with me in the middle of the night and was always close by to kiss and cuddle.

Aah well, I'm surviving it. And so is she. Growing up and going out on their own is part of the family plan, after all. When my kids can be self-sufficient in the world, I can feel a sense of pride that I've helped get them to that place. But as this last child blooms into adulthood, I'm especially grateful that I've developed other things to do with my time in addition to mothering.

Motherhood is undeniably the epitome of "the agony and the ecstasy." It's a role millions of us would fight through hell and high water to fulfill—a role that one in every ten women finds difficult, if not impossible, to achieve. If you're a mother, indulge yourself with some well-deserved pats on the back, and acknowledge the fact that you've taken on a tough but highly rewarding endeavor. The gratification you receive when your children are happy and healthy is hard to quantify, but I'm sure that like countless other women, you'll claim such gratification as the hallmark of your personal worth.

Respect yourself and other mothers for the enormously important job of nurturing our planet's future caretakers, and please accept praise from all of us for your invaluable participation in the circle of life.

Personal Tasks

- Appreciate your abilities as a mother.

- Forgive yourself; even mothers make mistakes. Do the best you can with the options on your plate.

- Be aware that you are a role model—you're teaching your children with your actions and behaviors every day, and they don't miss a trick.

- Be content as a person. Handle your responsibilities with dignity.

- Accept your own worth, and raise your children to respect and appreciate women *and* men as equals.

Wisdom from Your Peers

"When I sat down to type this out (which I'm doing ad lib as I go), I thought this would be easy, and I could just move through it. Actually, it has made me very thoughtful and has brought up many memories.

"My mother was strong and positive, and she played a huge role in making sure that her daughters felt worthy. My little town, with its excellent schools, added to that. I lived where, since there were few people, everyone counted; this 'men instead of women' thing didn't exist. Everyone was needed, so everyone was worthy. When I first came to the East Coast, I encountered a different attitude. It was shocking to me, and I felt angry. However, I just roll on. I believe many people here are shocked by me because I pay no attention to such nonsense—I just keep moving toward my goals.

"I learned that I could play an important part in presenting role models for young women (and men) in my work as a teacher. Once I found that I could be a teacher, and a good

one, my life settled into place. I could be a teacher at home, for my daughter; and I could be a teacher at school, for my students. I found a life and a career that gave me positive feedback every day of the week, every week of the year. I have so many 'moments' of worth as a result . . . so, so many: watching my daughter . . . watching my granddaughter—self-confident, with a strong sense of self-worth . . . watching my students do their work and seeing my alumni succeed in their lives and their work. I could write down a million examples.

"As I wrote these words, I thought about the teachers I had as a child; I also thought about my parents, who were wonderful, generous, kind, and intelligent people. I think that worth, for a man or a woman, has to grow out of parenting, teaching, and community goals. If those are put in place in childhood, then things work out. Inevitably, both men and women face mistakes, challenges, overwhelming disappointments, and some failures. But if the foundation is there, they will have a happy ending . . . or at least an ending that they can accept.

"Thanks for the chance to think about this.
It was a worthwhile thing for me to do."
— **Jeanine Basinger,** educator, Connecticut

"Watching my husband embrace fatherhood speaks to me about the value, worth, and power of being a woman. What an amazing gift to witness: your best friend/lover nurturing these tiny little spirits, created by your love, and sharing the responsibilities of parenthood. They say that 'Behind every

good man is a good woman.' Isn't the reverse true as well? And what a blessing for a woman to know that she can stand alone, but that she doesn't have to. I find that worth is measured by the quality of our relationships."
— **Alison Armstrong-Conner, Ph.D.;**
child psychologist; Ohio

"My mama personified 'grace.' She was loving and happy and provided me with enormous guidance. However, she lived in a time and place that did not encourage her to take her personal power. From the foundation she provided me, I've been able to claim and acknowledge my own worth and power. It's been (and continues to be) a journey of ups and downs, successes and extreme disappointments. But when I lose my footing or get knocked down, I work hard to get back up and find my balance—my power, my worth."
— **Tricia Dressler,** television producer, Georgia

"I recently had a difficult situation arise in my life. I found that rather than drowning in my anger or negativity, I was able to find a true place of peace and happiness that wasn't dependent on anyone else, not even my children. This was an incredible gift I was given in my life, and I feel grateful daily for all I have. I think that only a woman can reach inside and actually work as hard as one needs to, to change oneself into a positive person when one is feeling so much negativity. It's a wonderful test, and as a woman I was truly able to rise to the occasion and become stronger, wiser, and more powerful as a

result. Most important, I feel that I have so much more to give because I'm not at all self-absorbed. This experience has allowed me to have more self-esteem."
— **Evelyn H.;** mother, daughter, sister;
Republic of Panama

Journal Questions

♥ Does being a mother add to your sense of self-worth? Do you feel fulfilled in your role as a mom?

♥ Did your parenting skills evolve naturally? What would you do differently?

♥ Does your spouse/partner take an active role in the parenting of your children? If not, why?

♥ Are you prepared to allow your kids to differentiate away from you? What can you do to get ready for that transition?

Self-Worth Affirmations

W.O.R.T.H.
Wisdom
I trust my instincts.
I am a wonderful mother.

W.O.R.T.H.
Optimism
I see the beauty of life, and I share
this vision with my young.

W.O.R.T.H.
Responsibility
I am the most important teacher my children have,
and therefore I continue to learn more
about the world around me.

W.O.R.T.H.
Tenacity
I am leaving the world a better place for my kids.

W.O.R.T.H.
Honesty
I share my truth, and I help my children discover their own.

CHAPTER 9

Finances and Freedom:
Working for Independence

"Women fake orgasms and men fake finances."
— **Suze Orman,** financial consultant

Do you use your career, your job, or the work you do as a measuring tool to size up your worth? While it's a mistake to equate your value solely with money, you may have indeed been raised to do so, thanks to references to your "net worth" and the like. Therefore, you might be tempted to make assumptions about yourself based on what you *have,* rather than who you *are.* Make no mistake, who you are is the axis of your worth. Still, the *expression* of your worth is impacted if you have no control over what you have.

I'm sure you've discovered by now that personal experiences in your individual environment inform much of your behavior, and this includes decisions relating to your career path. The way you handle your finances is determined, at least in part, by what you've been taught and exposed to.

Ask yourself these questions:

- Did your mother stay at home, or did she work outside your house as well?

- Do you think that men and women should share household duties equally?

- Did your teacher tend to ask boys to answer the math questions when you were in school?

- Were you encouraged to study medicine, science, or engineering?

- Did you grow up planning to pursue a career in addition to having a family, or were you raised to think that the two were mutually exclusive?

- Were you taught to handle your own finances, or were they always controlled by someone else?

- As a young woman, did you learn about savings accounts, retirement plans, and insurance options? Did you assume that someone else would handle those aspects of your life?

A Woman's Work

Regardless of whatever messages you may have received as a little girl, know that women today not only want to bake the proverbial cake, but they want to eat a proper slice of it, too. Yet although we're making greater contributions to the workforce now than ever before, this old saying remains true: "Men may toil from sun to sun, but a woman's work is never done." The never-ending reality of 24/7 labor for females is particularly apparent for moms who work outside the home.

The fact that most women work long hours is not really the issue here—we're usually willing to burn the midnight oil when we want to accomplish something, and this applies to men as well. The problem is that men are usually *compensated* for the long hours they work. The contributions women make behind the scenes, however—such as housekeeping, meal preparation, and child care—are being made without monetary reimbursement.

How do you factor the value of those freebies into your net worth? Do you think that you should be paid for managing your household, or is your family's respect and appreciation enough? Do you and your spouse/partner place an appropriate value on your contributions at all? Keep in mind that one calculation suggests that at $22 an hour, stay-at-home moms who work approximately 91 hours per week would earn more than $130,000 if they were paid for that labor. Is your check in the mail? I didn't think so.

Society can't afford us . . . literally. If homemakers went on strike, society wouldn't be able to function as it does.

So how can we gain the respect and recompense we deserve for the contributions we make? That's a very good question, and the answer is: we're still working on it. In many nations, women can vote, race cars, assume the power as heads of state, and fly to outer space; yet despite the Herculean strides we've made, we're a long way from equalizing all of the discrepancies. Here in the United States, women make up nearly half of the workforce, yet we do *not* claim half of the wealth—we continue to grapple with financial equity and compensation for work supplied. Recent studies show that American women with college degrees still earn only 73 cents for every dollar that similarly educated men earn. With that kind of discrepancy, a 25-year-old college-educated woman would lose $523,000 in potential earnings over the course of her lifetime.

Around the globe, women are paid approximately 30 to 40 percent less than men for the same jobs; antiquated cultural constraints in some countries also tether many females to a difficult if not untenable existence in which they're not allowed to work outside the home, drive, travel freely, or attend school. In developing nations, where control is even more concentrated in the male zone, the blatant stratification of women persists—needless to say, enmeshed cultural schemas are strong.

The bottom line is this: women perform 66 percent of the world's work, yet we own only 1 percent of the world's land and receive only 11 percent of its income. Ironically, for all that work being done, a White House conference on aging found that 30 million female baby boomers won't be able to afford to retire. This is a statistic we should take *very* seriously.

Remember that recognition for the significance of your contributions and the validity of your participation in the overall economic stability of your life is an important factor in the development of your self-esteem.

Breaking the Glass Ceiling

Luckily, we *are* making progress. Women are making substantial gains in the career arena; in fact, women-owned businesses are growing at *twice* the rate of all U.S. firms.

We're breaking through the so-called glass ceiling all over the place. For example:

- There are 9.1 million women-owned businesses in the United States; 26 percent of them have home pages on the Internet.

- Women comprise 23 percent of the CEOs in America.

- Women are influencing home design: con-tractors, architects, and designers are paying attention to what we want because we outspend men on many technical gadgets, products, and appliances.

- Women care about what it takes to run an efficient home, so we're beginning to demand a voice in the decisions being made in that area.

- In 2004, women bought 47 percent of all paint-ing supplies and half of all bathtubs.

- Women outspend men $55 billion to $41 billion at Best Buy—a consumer-electronics retailer.

- Whether we're in charge of the checkbook or not, women influence 90 percent of the total purchases our families make.

Women do more than influence day-to-day expenditures and impact the design of cell phones, cameras, and home theaters; we've also taken charge of the "family vacation."

We make 70 percent of the travel decisions for our families, suggesting the necessity of an entirely new business model for the tourism industry. This trend certainly hasn't gone unnoticed, as more and more companies in the United States and elsewhere are waking up to the fact that if they overlook women, they do so at their own financial peril.

Based on the loud-and-clear earning-and-spending message we're sending, companies are reaching out to an increasingly female-centric consumer base that has more financial muscle and purchasing independence than ever before. Good. Let them woo us. We're here, we're strong, and we've got buying power. In fact, if we continue in our current trajectory, we'll be earning more money than men do by the year 2028. Now that's a prediction worth saluting! We'll have accomplished the unimaginable and cut a substantial wedge from the mother lode.

There's no doubt that women *should* be in the work-force and have more of a say over our resources. When we are, society benefits, as proven by Nobel Prize laureate Dr. Muhammad Yunus of Bangladesh. Dr. Yunus is the founder of Grameen Bank, and he discovered that by giving microcredit to impoverished women, they could change *entire* communities for the better. Through his efforts to help millions climb out of the grips of poverty, Dr. Yunus saw firsthand that giving opportunity to women was the best bet.

When I interviewed him for this book, he stated, "We saw that money going to women brought much more benefit to the family than money going to men. So we changed our policy and gave a high priority to women." As a result, 96 percent of the four million borrowers in Grameen Bank are women.

Although we've certainly not reached 50-50 earning capacity yet, some careers *have* reached parity in pay scale with men and have even tipped the scale in our favor. What a concept.

Warren Farrell, author of *Why Men Earn More: The Startling Truth Behind the Pay Gap—and What Women Can Do About It,* identified more than 80 occupations for which women were paid more than men in 2007. I've included a sampling from that list here:

FIELD	WOMEN	MEN
Sales engineers	$89,908	$62,660
Statisticians	$49,140	$36,296
Legislators	$43,316	$32,658
Speech-language pathologists	$45,136	$35,048
Motion-picture projectionists	$35,412	$27,924
Tool and die makers	$46,228	$40,144
Aerospace engineers	$78,416	$70,356
Radiation therapists	$59,124	$53,300
Human-resources assistants	$30,420	$28,028
Agricultural and food specialists	$41,704	$39,156
Advertising and promotions managers	$42,068	$40,144

The Importance of Financial Freedom

It's a fact that control over our own finances—the ability and wherewithal to provide for ourselves and handle our own money—is a crucial step toward establishing an equitable balance in society, as well as in achieving better overall outcomes for ourselves. Yet studies show that many of us are intimidated by finances and are reluctant to get our personal fiscal issues in order.

If we struggle with this problem, we must take the appropriate steps now, because the situation may deteriorate as we grow older. One of the biggest mistakes we can make is to remain ignorant about money. That's because:

- ♥ Anywhere from 80 to 90 percent of women today will be solely responsible for their own finances at some point in their lives.

- ♥ Women typically outlive men.

- ♥ The average midlife woman who's been through a divorce will remain single and earn an average income of less than $12,000.

- ♥ The health-care needs of women are greater than men; it's important to know how they're going to be paid for.

It may help to think about your financial status more in terms of the *independence* it affords you. A man is most certainly *not* a plan, since dependency breeds vulnerability. So, based on many indicators, including the fact you may

outlive the man in your life, it's vital for you to be fiscally aware; it's even more essential for you to be fiscally independent. I cannot stress this enough: *your need for financial freedom and know-how is especially vital as you age.*
Consider the following:

- Women migrate in and out of the job market to care for children and elderly parents—on average, this means that 15 percent of your career will be spent out of the workforce.

- For every year out of the workforce, you'll need to work *five* years to recover the lost income, promotion possibilities, and pension coverage.

- Two-thirds of the 7.2 million elderly women in America who live alone have incomes below $15,000.

- Social security is the *only source of income* for more than 25 percent of elderly women.

- Fifty percent of working women are in low-paying jobs with no pensions.

- Female retirees typically receive about half of the pension benefits that male retirees receive.

- Women over the age of 65 are twice as likely as men of the same age to live in poverty.

Speaking of poverty, if I wasn't in a position to help out my parents financially, there's a good chance that's what they'd be dealing with. And this is despite the fact that my dad worked for the telephone company for most of his working life, was always very frugal, has a pension, and collects social-security benefits. My mom also worked briefly—first as a riveter during the war and later at a small button shop in San Diego—but once she became pregnant with my brother, my dad carried the financial load. Both of my parents, who were relatively healthy during their younger years, are now experiencing complications with their health . . . but they're both in their 80s, so I suppose this comes with the territory.

Thank God they both still have each other, and that's a blessing our entire family treasures. But between health-care costs, the cost of gas, and the general increase in the cost of *everything,* my mother and father would have long ago plowed through their savings if they had to fend for themselves. (This scenario becomes catastrophic when applied to an 80-something woman who's alone, without family who can help, and with little or no resources of her own.)

May this serve as a lesson to learn and a warning to be heeded. I hope you see that in order to be better positioned for a happy old age, you need to maintain some personal control over your money and resources as soon as possible.

Building for the Future

A discussion about finances in a book celebrating a woman's worth may appear to put so much emphasis on fiscal solvency that you could argue in favor of the money-equals-worth equation. But I sincerely hope you don't reach this conclusion, because it's not my intent at all. Money doesn't buy you worth any more than it can buy you love. However, you'd be wise to recognize that a personal bank account—*your* money in the bank—gives you options that you don't have without it, such as freedom, autonomy, independence, and personal power.

At a critical time in my life when I was a single working mom with no retirement plan, no substantial savings, and limited financial options, my father gave me some sage advice: he astutely pointed out that I couldn't count on having a man's pension to sustain me when I reached retirement age. He was basing his information on the fact that I'd been through two divorces and my prospects seemed pretty dim. He correctly asserted that I needed to prepare for my retirement myself—*regardless of whether or not I'd again have a man in my life.*

My dad's observation was timely: I was in my midthirties and had yet to devise or even contemplate a long-term financial plan. Thankfully, he explained the concept of IRA accounts and gave me $50 to help me open one. From that point on, I had $25 a week direct deposited into my IRA account—while that may not sound like a lot, the fact that I was building my own retirement savings made me feel as if I were sitting on top of the world.

Having your own personal savings, checking, and retirement accounts allows you to make choices; you can be proactive about the course your life takes without needing to ask permission. It allows you to not only *feel* your worth, but also to *express* it in a way that mainstream society understands. In many ways, your economic currency helps establish your social currency. That being the case, the following can help you take more responsibility for your economic currency:

- Protect yourself by maintaining a marketable skill. Continue to learn—even when you must duck out of the job market periodically to have children or attend to other family responsibilities, you want to be able to jump back in when you're ready.

- Retain a financial advisor.

- Adhere to the basics of financial planning: spend less, save and invest more, and follow a plan.

- If you're married, keep an updated personal copy of your financial documents and know what your personal financial liabilities are. If your husband or partner declares bankruptcy, you could be forced to claim bankruptcy, too. What then?

- Make sure that you have adequate insurance coverage.

- Help yourself by taking some responsibility for your own future. Open a retirement account, such as a 401(k) or an IRA, and invest as much as you can in it.

Accept Responsibility

Coming to terms with your own finances and what part you'll play in supporting yourself is crucial, yet there could be confusion about this due to cultural schemas and expected male-female behaviors. It's time to consider a different paradigm that will include being fair about your participation. For example, chivalry and good manners are probably behaviors that you desire from men—but you may feel that if you don't pay your share for a dinner date, your male companion might expect something more than dessert at the end of the meal.

Alternatively, I'd be remiss if I didn't mention the fact that women raised to believe that men should pay for everything are conflicted when it comes to sharing their own salaries. This attitude and sense of entitlement, though perhaps understandable in an illogical way, perpetuates the "what's his is ours, and what's mine is mine" mind-set. Some specialists suggest that this attitude prevails because many women still carry out most of the domestic duties, even when both individuals have outside careers; thus, it gives them license to feel that more is "owed" to them.

The money juggle persists as a murky area in relationships: even today, couples' counselors report that one of the three most common arguments in relationships revolves around money (with sex and children being the other two). You can avoid such disputes by being aware of your perceptions and preconceived notions about financial matters, including how males and females are supposed to handle them. Be honest and open with your partner about your feelings and expectations regarding financial arrangements—*communicate.* And work out a harmonious budget that brings into balance *all* of the contributions *both* of you make to your life together.

These days, living expenses are such that dual salaries are necessary in order for most couples to achieve the goals they've set out for themselves, so many of them maintain an understanding from the beginning that they'll need to share the burden of financial liability.

Yet even though economic need may mean you *have* to work, I'm sure you'd agree that your vocation also brings you an important element of satisfaction and fulfillment. Most women who work outside the home say that despite the time constraints and the juggling of duties, they're happier and more personally satisfied when they can pursue their career passions. Their careers are so important, in fact, that many of them say that their self-worth is actually *enhanced* by them . . . I bet you can relate.

Regardless of whether you work outside the home or not, be very clear that when you take more responsibility for your own finances, your feelings of security and worth will increase exponentially . . . and *that's* a good thing.

Personal Tasks

♥ Get a clear understanding of your financial status. Calculate your net worth by adding up your cash assets, property, and personal belongings; and then subtract your debt, including home mortgage and credit cards, to get an instant idea of your net worth.

- ♥ Keep in mind this helpful general rule: a healthy net worth equals your age times 10 percent of your pretax income. What a wake-up call, eh?

- ♥ Manage and track your spending—you'll soon see where you overindulge.

- ♥ Start a savings account, and save as much as you can. You'll need it, trust me.

- ♥ Reduce credit-card spending. (Duh.)

- ♥ Ask for a raise. (Duh again.)

- ♥ Plan in advance for retirement by opening an IRA or participating in a 401(k).

- ♥ Spend less and enjoy more. Think green—it's *in* to be more consumer conscious now.

- ♥ Be reasonable with yourself: if you can only save a little, then save a little. Remember the old adage that "if you put a little on a little, soon you will have a lot."

Wisdom from Your Peers

"After three months of working in a company, my boss who was an accountant mentioned to me that I had to resign because the company could no longer afford my salary . . . and I believed him. I went to thank the top executives for

the opportunity they gave me and for the experience
that I got during those months working for them,
and they were surprised that I'd resigned.

"The next day we all had a meeting, and my boss said that
I was not doing the job as I should—I realized after a few
days that he really wanted to hire his lover. The top
executives knew I was a hard worker and decided I should
keep my job. It was a challenge for me because I had to see
my old boss every day. He could have told me the truth . . .
I knew I was capable of getting another job. He made me
work extra hours every day—I was also doing his work,
but I didn't care because I was learning bookkeeping.
After three years, I became his boss. There was an audit,
and when the top executives found out that he
wasn't honest, they made him resign."
— **Georgina Garcia Ricano,** estate manager, Mexico

"I have a male boss who is rather difficult and runs
a dictatorship in this office. It's impossible to confront him
about anything. I found that the reason I butted heads
with him so much is because I tried to approach him on an
equal level, returning his attacks and irrational statements
with equally impatient bursts. So I changed my tactics—
now I try to invoke my feminine intuition, my motherly
side, by reasoning with him lovingly and trying to
appeal to his own femininity."
— **Estefania,** Colombia

*"I'd built a unique company from concept to manufacturing
to marketing, with offices in New York, Los Angeles, and
Paris. Sales were at capacity in the first year, and my
three most important competitors were all trying to buy
my company. I felt a little out of my league to negotiate the
sale, so my husband (who's a film producer) and a battery
of lawyers worked out the details and took care of
the negotiations. Meanwhile, I was flying all over
the world keeping the company growing.*

*"After almost nine months of intense negotiations, all parties
were to sign off on the sale at 6 P.M. on a Friday evening in
New York, yet there were several outstanding points that were
important to me that hadn't been conceded by the buyer.
By 4 A.M. the deal looked like it was off, and the lawyers
started packing their briefcases. I turned to the buyer and
suggested that the two of us talk 'sans' lawyers.*

*"When we closed the office door, I took out a little aqua
Tiffany box and handed it to him, saying that I wanted
him to have something to remember this date whether the
sale went through or not. He looked at me in disbelief.
He then left the room; when he returned, he also had a little
aqua Tiffany box. We both opened the boxes at the same
time . . . and it turned out that we'd given each other
a similar gift with a phrase and the date of the closing
engraved on it. I'd given him a sterling key chain with a
whistle attached; on a small disc, I'd had the date engraved
along with the world <u>ultreya</u>, which means 'move forward
with courage.' His gift to me was the same whistle, but in gold
and on a chain; his engraved message included the closing
date and the phrase, 'Whistle if you need me.'*

*"We looked at each other, and he turned away so that
I couldn't see his face—but I'd already noted the tears in
his eyes. We discussed the points I was holding on to,
and he ceded all of them, feeling that this deal was meant
to happen. At this moment, I felt worthy of all the things
I've ever believed in for myself, and that I was truly a
capable and talented woman."*
— **Elaine K.,** marketing entrepreneur, Ohio

*"I think that kids are growing up with working mothers more
and more, so I think there are many more role models. I hope
we can instill in them that to make their own living and create
their own freedom of choice by being financially independent
is a gift. Doing it on their own will give them such joy."*
— **Martha Luttrell,** entertainment agent, Canada

Journal Questions

- What compensation do you receive for the work you do at home? Is it equitable? If not, what would you change?

- Are you dependent upon others for your livelihood? What can you do to buck up your own financial security?

- Are you comfortable with the salary you're receiving? If not, when will you ask for a raise?

♥ What can you do to feel more in control of your finances?

Self-Worth Affirmations

W.O.R.T.H.
Wisdom
I know that financial independence
ensures certain freedoms.

W.O.R.T.H.
Optimism
I am capable and highly talented.

W.O.R.T.H.
Responsibility
I am assertive. I have abilities that serve me well.

W.O.R.T.H.
Tenacity
I am determined! I contribute to my financial well-being.

W.O.R.T.H.
Honesty
I admit my vulnerabilities,
and I know that I can build on my strengths.

CHAPTER 10

Health and Happiness: Choosing the High Road of Harmony

"Happiness is an expression of the soul in considered actions."
— **Aristotle**

I'd like you to spend just a moment to honestly take your "mood temperature." Would you say you're happy? Have you wondered if happiness is a relative state? Is it a right, an ethereal emotion, or a reaction to circumstances? Are women—oh, okay, are *all* humans—equally capable of accessing and maintaining it, or is it distributed willy-nilly by fate?

Although happiness can mean different things to different people, it tends to refer to the experience of joy, contentment, or positive well-being . . . combined with a sense that life is good, meaningful, and worthwhile. But how can that lofty goal be reached? Are happy, healthy people born with all the luck or do they just *seem* more successful and empowered? Does financial success have anything to do with it?

As you're most assuredly aware by now, having money doesn't ensure happiness—there are plenty of rich people walking around who are miserable and cranky. While wealth can be one of the line items in a list of achievements and can certainly provide a sense of security and comfort, happiness is more *a state of mind* than a balance sheet of possessions or accomplishments.

Even though happiness is relative and subjective, joyful people do have a lot in common. Studies show that such individuals are generally:

- Comfortable with who they are
- Devoted to friends and family, and they nurture those relationships
- Optimistic about the future
- Grateful for what they have and comfortable with their ambitions
- Kind and helpful—they give to charities and practice random acts of kindness
- Health conscious and partake in regular exercise
- Committed to lifelong goals
- Resilient—they bounce back when times get rough
- Secure in their ability to effect changes in their lives
- Self-assured

How many of the above items can you check off in the affirmative? If your happiness temperature is running low, you need to make some changes.

It's All in Your Head

Although ignorance can sometimes be bliss, even if you've been around the block a few times—that is, you've experienced your share of woe or lived in extremely compromising situations—you can find ways to be happy. Taking responsibility for your own contentment may seem like an overwhelmingly large task, but the spark to do so is actually quite small and can be found right in your own head.

Studies in cognitive behavioral therapy reveal that you can manage your own thoughts and feelings; it's a decision you make. In other words, you can choose not to allow your interior mental filter to disqualify the positive things in your life.

A subtle shift in your intentions and thought patterns lets happiness bloom where discord was growing only moments before. Positive action begets positive action, and it's contagious: smiles and laughter create more smiles and laughter. If you're a skeptic, use yourself as the test subject in an experiment and do what happy people do—you'll notice immediate changes in the way you feel.

For example, try the following:

- ♥   Choose to be happy. Find something in your life or the world that's beautiful, joyous, kind, and wondrous; and focus on it. (For example, *The sky is blue today, and the color is glorious.*)

- ♥   Be grateful for what you have.

- ♥   Imagine your glass as half full, and be optimistic that you're capable of filling it to the top.

- ❤ Express your good intentions in thought and action.

- ❤ Avoid social comparisons—rather than habitually comparing yourself with others, live your *own* life well.

- ❤ Trust that the universe will work to bring you what you put your attention on—be sure to think about and project the good things, rather than allowing yourself to dwell on the bad.

- ❤ Laugh, smile, and appreciate humor.

- ❤ Give yourself a break. Happiness is not about seeking perfection—it has more to do with recognizing that you're perfect just as you are.

Studies show that systematic self-help speeds recovery, that happiness is actually the cure for unhappiness. While that sounds oxymoronic, it's a legitimately true statement. Again, you must *choose* to be happy to overcome discontent. When you come to terms with your persona, with your place on the planet, and ultimately with *your life,* you'll certainly be more content than individuals who feel that fate has dealt them a rotten hand.

If you find that trying to fix everyone else's life has made you too busy to discern where your own joy resides, try resigning from being "general manager of the universe" for a moment—instead, allow your life to unfold as it was meant to. Although having personal control of the course of your life is important, don't think that you need to micromanage *everything.* Trust that the universe will support you in a positive way once you put that message out there. You can find *something* to be happy about, even if everything around you is spinning out of control.

Take a cue from watching kids, since they have the uncanny ability to laugh no matter what's going on around them. If you want to see pure resiliency and courage at work, visit the cancer ward of any children's hospital, and you'll be humbled. Kids who are battling life-threatening diseases and facing seemingly hopeless circumstances are often much stronger than the adults charged with caring for them. Remarkably, many of these boys and girls seem to find ways to entertain themselves and enjoy happy moments as they come.

Think of children when you get too bogged down with gloom; and let your own innocent, joyous inner child come out and play.

The Power of Belief

Belief in yourself and your ability to take control of your experiences doesn't mean that you're a *solipsist,* one who adheres to a theory that the self is all that can be known to exist. Now I'm not suggesting that you won't be affected by the actions of others in your pursuit of happiness; however, the issue of faith—both in God and in yourself—does come into play here. Your *belief* that you can effect positive change is a major initial step.

Making the leap of faith that's required to take charge of your well-being, your self-worth, and your happiness can seem daunting, if not impossible. Yet even if you've learned over time that events and circumstances are in charge of the way you feel, research proves that you need to reconsider this notion.

Studies show that life outcomes are a combination of influences configured, as you may have guessed, by the nurturing (or lack of it) that you received in your childhood and by your environment. However, you still have a lot to say *personally* about your happiness.

In her book *The How of Happiness,* Sonja Lyubomirsky suggests that there's a scientific formula that describes where your contentment comes from. The formula works out as follows: 50 percent of your ability to be happy comes to you via your genetically determined set points; in other words, what you've inherited from your parents. Another 10 percent comes from your environment; that is, situations you encounter in your life, where you live, and so forth. But here's a salient bit of data that you don't want to miss: a whopping *40 percent* of your ability to be happy is due to *your own intentions,* meaning your behavior. Obviously you'll want to take this 40 percent quite seriously.

Granted, you can't change your past, and your present situation may seem daunting. But your future depends in great part on how you *behave, think,* and *feel* about yourself today. Your endeavors may test your mettle, but each time you meet a challenge, you get stronger and *happier.* And lest you forget, in terms of evolution, survival of the fittest is a recurring theme. Essentially, you hold the key to your own happiness.

If you want to keep a genuine smile on your face and take advantage of that 40 percent of influence, practice the following regularly:

♥ Express gratitude.

♥ Nurture your feelings of optimism.

♥ Resist overthinking (ruminating) and comparing yourself with others.

♥ Practice random acts of kindness.

♥ Nurture your social relationships.

♥ Develop coping skills.

♥ Learn to forgive.

♥ Engage in activities that provide you with flow experiences (refer back to Chapter 4).

♥ Delight in life's joys.

♥ Create goals for yourself and commit to them.

♥ Nurture your body, mind, and soul.

Happy People Are Healthier

Do you realize that your ability to feel joy and contentment affects your mental *and* physical health? To that end, one of the most intriguing treatment interventions for cancer patients is humor. When such individuals watch funny movies or listen to comedians who make them laugh, a remarkable thing happens: they become more receptive to their treatments and medications. Even when things look bleak and the *quantity* of life is endangered, a positive outlook has an enormous impact on the *quality* of life. Humor is an exceptionally strong medicine.

Of course, attaining and sustaining happiness doesn't guarantee that you'll never be sad or discouraged or face challenges. Challenges are part of human existence; surmounting them is what strengthens your foundation and augments your growth. While major concerns naturally require your attention and proactive behavior, the popular saying "Don't sweat the small stuff" is worth adopting as a mantra because fretting over trivial annoyances is nerve-wracking. Burrowing yourself too deeply into life's many little pitfalls and disappointments is not only stressful, but it's also a waste of time and energy. Practice envisioning a broader view, because your ability to see the big picture will serve you well.

My mother is 83 years young, and based on her current health status, you'd probably understand if I told you that she is grumpy and resentful. She's had two hip replacements, two knee replacements, and two back surgeries. She has lost eight inches in height over the years, has type 2 diabetes and osteoporosis, and is in chronic pain from arthritis. But my mom, God bless her, is constantly smiling. She's sweet to everyone, and my girlfriends claim that she's the best hugger in town. She isn't thrilled about not being able to drive anymore, nor does she like the fact that she needs a walker or cane to get around; but she still swims, giggles, and gets a thrill out of each day. Her joyous attitude gives her a quality of life that might not exist if she were to allow depression and sadness to fill her mind.

Take a page from my mom's book and learn to make lemonade out of life's lemons:

- Avoid nit-picking and paying too much attention to the small annoyances of life.

- Focus on the good things around you. (Surely you can identify at least a few!)

- Deal with sadness and disappointment with an aura of curiosity—try to find the light at the end of the tunnel and the lesson in the hardship, and then move forward.

- Realize that your efforts to find the silver lining in life's trials and difficulties *will* pay off.

Coping with Stress and Depression

Stress is inevitable in life, and sometimes it can be overwhelming. Essentially the product of unresolved fear and anger, stress suppresses and damages the integrity and function of your immune system, thus jeopardizing your ability to ward off sickness. It basically throws an uncomfortable wet blanket all over you.

Depression and other illnesses can then result, and they require biomedical and/or psychological attention. (By the way, genetics plays a part in this: studies suggest that depression can run in families, is more common in women, and usually starts between the ages of 15 and 30.) Please excuse the expression, but it's a depressing thought that an estimated *20 million* people in the United States suffer from this disorder.

Do be on the alert if you feel your life spinning out of control or if someone in your family has been diagnosed with depression. If you're in the midst of a particularly rocky patch in life, or if you're in the recovery process from a physical or mental illness, make sure that you formulate a support plan you can employ when you feel your self-control or ability to cope withering. Call it your "911 plan," and keep it on a laminated card in your wallet. Your plan should include the phone numbers of three friends or family members whom you trust completely and a couple of stress-relieving, *grounding* behaviors—such as sitting in a chair with both feet on the ground and initiating deep abdominal breathing.

Now don't panic as you're reading this chapter. *Not everyone who feels depressed is suffering from depression.* Life is a journey that has ups and downs, and I'm sure you're doing the best you can to navigate them. However, if you suspect that you *are* suffering from depression, please don't hide away. The National Institute of Mental Health has made consistent efforts to reduce the stigma that's often associated with mental illness, and it sends the clear message that help and healing are possible. Know that you're not alone, and that there are viable interventions available to help you get your*self* and your *life* back on track.

If you're curious about what symptoms are indicative of depression, answer the following questions. They're personal in nature, of course, but as far as I know, nobody is recording your thoughts, so you can make your disclosures in private. Your answers will provide insight into your feelings and state of mind. So:

__ Are you feeling sad and moody?

__ Does your future seem hopeless?

__ Do you think you're a failure?

__ Do you feel worthless, inadequate, or inferior?

__ Are you self-critical and do you feel guilty?

__ Do you blame yourself for everything?

__ Do you have trouble making decisions?

__ Are you irritable, resentful, and frustrated?

___ Have you lost interest in activities that used to engage you or lost touch with family and friends?

___ Do you feel overwhelmed and unmotivated?

___ Do you dislike the way you look?

___ Do you have a poor self-image?

___ Has your appetite changed dramatically?

___ Are you having a difficult time sleeping or have your sleep patterns changed?

___ Have you lost the desire for sex?

___ Do you worry about your health a lot?

___ Have you had thoughts that life isn't worth living?

If you answered yes to more than two of these questions, do yourself a favor and seek outside support from a qualified mental-health professional. You deserve to be happy, and with the right support, I'm convinced that you can be.

A Foundation of Strength

Naturally we all wish that our lives could be happy, healthy, and stress free; yet chances are that if we live long enough, we'll face adversity, health issues, and stress. Our relationships are obviously not immune: studies suggest that close to half of the U.S. population will experience one severe traumatic event during their lifetime. (And by the way, divorce is considered traumatic.)

How you handle the good *and* difficult times in your relationships and your life in general is reflective of the foundation of strength you've built within yourself. You can access such strength when you need it most by drawing upon your coping skills. If you don't know what they are, consider these examples:

- **Problem-solving coping**—you concentrate on doing something about the problem, making a plan of action, and coming up with strategies.

- **Emotion-focused coping**—you neutralize your negative emotions by positively reinterpreting the situation or by using relaxation methods.

- **Posttraumatic growth**—you feel that you've learned from the situation and are stronger because of it. As Friedrich Nietzsche said, "That which does not kill me, makes me stronger."

- **Finding meaning and using thought disputation**—you rethink assumptions about how life is *supposed* to work, disputing or challenging your own pessimistic or distorted thoughts.

- **Social support**—you reach out to relatives, friends, lovers, clergy, or physicians for advice.

- **Exercise**—believe it or not, this is an extremely beneficial way of coping with stress. Studies show that three brief workouts a week will improve your health and elevate your mood; physical exercise is a sure way to raise your happiness temperature.

Women are very often the organizers and conductors of everyone else's happiness and contentment. We're geared to nurture and protect our children and to be of service to our mates and friends, often to the point of forgetting and neglecting our *own* needs. It's easy to see why so many of us feel as if our self-worth comes from our ability to make everyone else feel fulfilled.

Yet it turns out that women who accept and appreciate themselves and express their self-worth are happier than those who chronically struggle with esteem and existential issues. So what's their secret? Faith in possibility is one of the keys. Try pretending that you're a sculptor who can look at a large piece of marble and see a masterpiece within it. *You're* that masterpiece—when you see yourself that way, you're more likely to have joy in your heart.

While it may be contrary to your upbringing or to your culture, remember that your own health and happiness are just as important as anyone else's. Pay attention to these vital, fundamental aspects of your life . . . and just in case you forgot, *you're worth the effort!*

You can take credit for attracting happiness; you could call it fate; or you can choose to base it on your religious beliefs and prayer—it doesn't particularly matter. As the saying goes, "A coincidence is God's way of remaining anonymous." Whatever path you take to happiness, as long as you realize that you're partly responsible for your direction and your destination, you'll be on the right road. As all those who have recovered from an illness or an addiction have discovered, seeing new horizons rather than dead ends is uplifting and exhilarating. It's wind beneath your wings. You *can* be happy.

The reality of this new mind-set can be a thermal rush like you've never known. What are you waiting for? Spread those wings of yours and fly. . . .

Personal Tasks

In order to take charge of your happiness, I suggest that you follow this 12-step, recovery-of-self-worth, yes-I-can-be-happy plan:

1. Evaluate the domains of your life—such as career, hobbies, motherhood, marriage/partnership, and friendships—and seek to nourish each one.

2. Take charge of your health—make good nutrition and physical fitness a priority. Statistics show that women's life spans are increasing, so make sure that the quality of your life keeps up with the quantity.

3. If you haven't already done so, open a personal bank account for your own private savings. Save money every week, and start a retirement account as well.

4. Make it your business to understand your financial status. If you're a stay-at-home mom, participate in budget planning and carve out an amount that's for your own private use.

5. Seek support from a compassionate listener— be it a therapist, trusted friend, or mentor— to help you work through your challenges.

6. Initiate open communication with your partner/ mate/spouse and discuss the dynamics of your

relationship. Tell the truth about your needs, desires, goals, and problems.

7. Know your own story—where you started, where you are, and where you want to go. Stay abreast of global happenings and come up with your own opinion about them.

8. Determine to assert yourself, and accept authority in an activity in your life. Take responsibility, and feel the positive energy you get when you accomplish what you've set out to do.

9. Plot out some future, achievable goals— what would you like to see yourself doing in one, two, or five years? What steps do you need to take to get there?

10. Learn a new skill and engage in new activities. Learn to swim, go mountain biking, ski, or take a finance or language class . . . the sky's the limit.

11. Network—make an effort to interact with like-minded individuals, particularly women. Share what you know, and learn from others.

12. Seek support from all available sources in order to achieve happiness and a positive sense of esteem and self-worth. The Internet is full of information, and if you desire that tactile connection, go to your local library—bibliotherapy is a valid, recognized tool for self-help.

Wisdom from Your Peers

"A woman is the one who grows and makes everybody grow happy around her. She's a great mother, a great spouse, and a great worker. She's leading the life she chooses to have for herself; she's a true great leader, but a silent one."
— **Galit Dayan,** marketing, Israel

"When my children were growing up, a friend who was a social worker convened a group of mothers and daughters who varied in age, religion, and racial backgrounds. We sat for hours in a number of sessions discussing what it meant to be a woman and how that has changed over time. It was one of the most rewarding and broadening activities I've ever had the privilege of participating in. We came from such different places and had very different ideas, yet there was a stunning commonality of maximizing potential through loving interaction. My daughter remembers it vividly, even though it was almost 20 years ago. I wish there were more opportunities to openly discuss the mystique of womanhood."
— **Sandra Duncan Holmes,** New York

"My children's father and I were divorcing. It was very difficult for my family, my friends, and my community (we live in a small town, so it was very public). My ex had brought a girlfriend to the house as soon as the kids and I had moved out. It was Christmas with all its trappings; the children were young teens and very uncomfortable knowing that their father would want them to come over for Christmas Eve and

bring presents for his girlfriend. It was just making them sick. However, they didn't want to stay home and risk damaging their relationship with their dad—so I went out and bought a dinner certificate for my ex, and the kids and I made a big flower arrangement for his girlfriend. The children were so relieved and grateful, and I was grateful that my actions helped them get through this difficult time. After all, the divorce wasn't about <u>them</u>, and they needed support and comfort. (As they got older, it turns out that they chose not to be a part of their father's life to the degree he expected.)

"I think my 'worth,' or what makes me feel good, is when I can make someone else's day better than they expected by giving them just a little extra attention, a compliment, or the like. The positive energy multiplies and spreads to others."
— **Jo Ann Ralston,** administrative assistant, Oregon

"When I was pregnant with my second child, I had a nanny who'd left her three-year-old son behind in her hometown. She used to take care of my two-year-old as if he was her own. I caught her crying more than one time, but she only had love and smiles for my family. She was a registered accountant in Peru, but she never had the means to validate her studies in the U.S., nor could she bring her son here.

"As I was enjoying every smile and new word my children learned, my nanny was missing her son. She couldn't return to her hometown because she had an abusive husband— so I told her that I'd help her with attorney fees so she could finalize her divorce, get custody of her son, and bring him here. She was so fantastic with my kids, but I knew

I was going to lose her once her son was here. Even so,
it was more important to me to help this suffering
mother than to think of my loss.

"It took less than a year for her to be able to see her son
again. It had been so long, and she was so scared! She
thought he would reject her—and it did take about a year
for him to forgive her for abandoning him. That was four
years ago. Since then, both of them have become citizens
of the United States; she's the manager of a retail store;
and he's a fantastic student. She phones me often, and
her calls remind me that there are a lot of people out there
who need just a little help to turn their lives around.
That made me feel worthy, because I know that
her story could have been very different."
— **Gabriela Teissier Lunetta,** journalist, Mexico

"At first, I'm tempted to define one's worth as a person's level
of confidence and pride. It's the ability to know that what you
contribute to this world matters. It's to believe that your words
are respected and your actions appreciated. It's the sense of
pride people feel when their accomplishments make them
better individuals. By 'better,' I mean 'more evolved.'"
— **Jillian Manus,** media agent, New York

Journal Questions

♥   Are you a happy person? If not, why?

- Does your happiness depend on the actions of others?

- Do you spend much of your time *organizing* happiness for others in your life? What can you do to ensure your own happiness?

Self-Worth Affirmations

W.O.R.T.H.
Wisdom
I value myself. I am unique, amazing, and worthy.

W.O.R.T.H.
Optimism
I am happy. I choose to enjoy my life, and I am creating a life to be happy with.

W.O.R.T.H.
Responsibility
I manage my own environment.

W.O.R.T.H.
Tenacity
I stay on course and remain true to myself.

W.O.R.T.H.
Honesty
I am willing to project my self-worth.

PART III

Giving Back: Sharing Your Wisdom

"It is easier to live through someone else than to become complete yourself. The freedom to lead and plan your own life is frightening if you have never faced it before. It is frightening when a woman finally realizes that there is no answer to the question 'who am I,' except the voice inside herself."
— from *The Feminine Mystique,* by **Betty Friedan**

"According to Buddhism, individuals are masters of their own destiny. And all living beings are believed to possess the nature of the Primordial Buddha Samantabhadra, the potential or seed of enlightenment, within them. So our future is in our own hands. What greater free will do we need?"
— **the Dalai Lama**

"Love life, engage in it, give it all you've got. Love it with a passion, because life truly does give back, many times over, what you put into it."
— **Maya Angelou**

"Personal relationships make a woman worthy. We are defined by how we feel about ourselves and how we make others feel in our presence. A worthy woman has self-esteem and gives back to society."
— **Sherry Lansing,** philanthropist, Illinois

CHAPTER 11

Celebrate Yourself: Acceptance and Appreciation

"Somehow we learn who we really are
and then live with that decision."
— **Eleanor Roosevelt**

What comes to mind when someone suggests that you "celebrate yourself"? Does your interior voice reply snidely, *Yeah, sure, just as soon as I pick up the dry cleaning, grab the kids from day care, and make dinner, I'll throw myself a party.* Does the idea of focusing on numero uno sound overly narcissistic? Perhaps celebrating yourself is so far down on your to-do list that it barely gets noticed except on your birthday.

The idea I'm proposing here obviously isn't necessarily about parties per se (although such festivities are certainly worthy and enjoyable)—it has more to do with embracing, accepting, and expressing yourself. Think of it this way: your celebration of you is actually the ability to see yourself as being *whole;* it's the gratifying exercise of acknowledging your full potential.

When you can appreciate yourself as a complete, irrevocably worthwhile person, you've *arrived.* You've figured out how to navigate the expectations, restrictions, and limitations of a cultural vision that seeks to prescribe the roles or definitions of what a woman is *supposed* to be; and despite those expectations, you've found your *own* niche. And that achievement, my friend, is definitely cause for celebration, because so many women struggle with the notion of loving themselves as they are.

Acceptance and Appreciation

Appreciating yourself—acknowledging your contributions and being comfortable with who you are—requires you to admit your sense of *efficacy,* or your ability to produce a desired effect. Personal power stems from the knowledge that you're worthwhile, effective, and vital; and that you can change your life. This mind-set is what drives you to achieve; to grow; to advocate; and, ultimately, to give back to a society that desperately needs your input.

You need to have a sense of personal power (that is, personal *intention*) to thrive and survive. This has nothing to do with brute force—that's another concept entirely, and not one that you were genetically wired for. Your testosterone levels are generally too low for that. No matter . . . you have other skills, and *lots* of other hormones.

Your true strength as a woman is much more cerebral than physical. If you remember the *Star Wars* movies and the concept of "the Force," you'll recall that Luke Skywalker was told he needed to find the Force within himself. Yoda never doubted that it was there, but Luke wasn't so sure. In the end, when Luke trusted himself, his inner power prevailed. I'm happy to be your Yoda *and* your Obi-Wan Kenobi. I don't doubt that your Force exists—I *know* it does, and I join you in celebrating it.

Tap into your inner strength. Assess your life, goals, values, and self-worth. Challenge yourself to take on whatever life throws at you, and then become more resilient by having faith and trust in yourself. And then you'll feel like celebrating who you are, not just on your birthday, but *every* day.

Try the following:

- Think about the things you're passionate about—your desires, likes, wishes, and talents— and write down your top five.

- Enlarge your vision of life—look beyond your usual vantage point to cultivate an awareness that there are other perspectives worth seeing.

- Take responsibility for the life you're living; that is, *the life you've created.* Choose it— acknowledge that your actions got you where you are. Decide to be happy . . . and to do things that *make* you happy.

- Balance your work with play, which is something that women and men of all ages need. You'll greatly benefit from the restorative value playtime brings you: you'll de-stress, and your brain will have a chance to work with different neural pathways . . . always a stimulating experience.

- ♥ Strengthen your body's automatic healing system by getting enough rest and exercise, as well as by eating a healthy diet that contains plenty of fresh produce. (Okay, you've heard this before, but it's true, and it will make quite a difference in how you feel.)

- ♥ Volunteer your time, talents, and/or treasure. *Give.*

- ♥ Prevent illness by caring for your physical and mental health. Reduce stress by cultivating a garden, adopting a pet, and journaling.

Personal Intentions

Have you noticed that one of the common denominators of fulfilled and contented people is personal intention? I've mentioned this before, but it's such an important point that it warrants repeating. Read this slowly so it can sink in: *in order to be a happy and successful person, you must cultivate happy and successful habits; one of those habits is the ability to feel good in your own skin—to have self-esteem no matter what your particular circumstances at any given moment.* Imagine self-esteem in this context as including a genuine liking of yourself; a calm, relaxed certainty that you can count on.

That inner drive of yours—let's call it your intention, the source of the energy you conjure up to complete your long list of workaday tasks—is one of the most potent tools you have. Use it to appreciate yourself (that is, your ideas, creations, beauty, strength, validity, and worth) every day.

There's nothing more beautiful than the recognition of your own potential. Come up with a little more vigor at the end of the day before you tumble into bed to value your part in the grand scheme of things, to acknowledge your input, and to *express gratitude* for it.

Are you capable of making changes, both subtle and substantial, to make way for self-care and self-appreciation in your life? Are you addressing these issues now? Ask yourself how often you employ the following:

- Positive self-talk; repeating affirmations
- The Law of Attraction—giving energy and attention to what you *want and desire* in life
- The purging of frustration—releasing the "hurts" in your life to make way for more satisfaction
- Acknowledging successes and taking credit for them
- Evaluating your progress and setting attainable goals

Your worth isn't confined to the trappings of life, the rules of life, or the associations in life. It is, however, a bona fide treasure, one that you must *regularly* acknowledge and appreciate. How do you go about doing so? Give some thought to these suggestions:

— **Stay true to yourself;** retain your independence in thought and spirit. You're obviously part of a community, and that's vital to your survival—but don't forget, even for a moment, that your own, individual input is *essential* and *valuable.*

— **Be willing to change the status quo.** The culture you're a part of, along with the society you live in, dictate what's expected of you—but *you* can decide what's most beneficial, nurturing, and life sustaining for you. Be open to change.

— **Continually learn**—retain a willingness to adapt to, and accommodate, the new.

— **Take an active role in your finances,** and be personally responsible for yourself. This is not to say that you should refuse partnerships and collaborations, since family systems are important and require teamwork. However, as part of your personal celebration, be aware that you're an integral participant in the economic system of your life, and maintain some control.

— **Think long term.** Prepare for what lies ahead so that each stage of your life will hold promise, yet try to experience every moment of the here-and-now . . . for in a very real sense, this is *all* you can be sure of.

Avoiding "Musterbation"

Narrow your focus from the big picture of everything you do in your life for a moment; instead, tune in to the personal, more intimate realm of yourself. That is, I'd like you to take a break from itemizing all the things you think you "must" do, which noted psychologist Albert Ellis calls "musterbation." *Should* and *must* statements generate way too much emotional turmoil in your life, so avoid them. Instead, reach for positive alternatives to consider by reminding yourself of the things you *have* accomplished and the goals you *are* working on. Turn ruminations of *I wish I had* or *I should have done* into *I wonder what will challenge me today, and I wonder how I'll handle it.*

Self-care shouldn't be an add-on or an afterthought, and you needn't feel like you're being overly selfish when you take care of yourself. Think of such care as being essential—focusing on your personal well-being is necessary and beneficial for your quality of life. Okay, I realize that siphoning time away from the tasks that must be completed for daily survival seems like an unreachable or even irresponsible dream. But if you don't spend time on yourself, the consequences can be quality-of-life threatening.

Slowing down long enough to play with your children, read a novel, or plant bulbs in your garden will not only pay benefits in the long run, they'll give you joy in the moment. And again, please remember that this moment is all you can be certain of.

Take a deep, long breath through your nose right now and slowly exhale through your mouth as you consider trying the following:

- ♥ Set aside a few minutes for yourself every day to reflect on things about yourself and the world you live in that you're thankful for.

- ♥ Acknowledge your achievements, big and small. For example, *I finished a chapter on my new book . . . I have a wonderful marriage and family . . . I took my second flying lesson . . . I shared my opinion with my boss . . . I potty trained my toddler,* and so forth.

- ♥ Allow yourself to change your routine by adding an interesting new activity, reading a different type of book, taking a walk at lunchtime with a friend, or what have you.

♥ Call your husband or partner in the middle of the day just to say "I love you."

♥ Fit exercise and good nutrition into your life in inventive ways: Stand on your tiptoes in the checkout line of the grocery store. Eat a vegetarian meal one night a week. Get up and move around every 15 minutes or so. And don't forget to stretch!

♥ Stand up for something! Get interested in the political system that guides your world: determine a social ill that you'd like to see changed, and then be part of the movement to change it.

Treat Yourself As the Beloved Child You Are

In order to be a self-confident woman, it is vital that you *express* that confidence. Yet since you've been trained to be a giver, nurturer, and comforter, the idea that you can actually come first—rather than second, third, or last—can be a high hurdle to jump. But jump anyway! Find that sweet spot in life: the position that feels harmonious and balanced; the place where not only are you appreciated by others for the gifts you bring to the table, but you also appreciate yourself without a guilty sensation that you've let some other important task slide when you do. *Acknowledge* and *appreciate* every step you take, baby, because the ground beneath your feet is hallowed.

In 1927, Indiana lawyer Max Ehrmann wrote "Desiderata" (which comes from a Latin word that means "things to be desired"), in an apparent desire to leave a precious yet humble gift to humankind. The poem beautifully and simply describes what Ehrmann felt most individuals would find desirous for a happy and fulfilling life, and it's well worth your reading from time to time.

Not only are you a child of the universe beloved by God, but as is so eloquently stated in "Desiderata," you have a *right* to be here. In fact, it's more than a right—your presence is *vital*. You represent all women in that you're the *portal* through which all human beings must arrive on the planet. That's a pretty important role, don't you agree?

Thus:

- Be grateful for who you are and what you do.

- Treat yourself with respect and dignity.

- Realize that you're a vital part of the circle of life. Humanity as we know it cannot survive without you.

- Walk proud and *be* equal.

I realize that this may seem self-indulgent, as if you're tooting your own horn. Perhaps you'd feel more comfortable asking yourself, "How can I use my abilities and an appreciation of myself to make my life better?" Framed this way, you might answer that when you tap into your inner strength, you can imagine options rather than roadblocks.

It's much more difficult to imagine possibility when your personal strength and assets are exhausted.

Take a moment now to think about what kinds of things you can do to make your life better today. Here are some tips to get you started:

1. Define your own core values, and determine how you can incorporate these values into your daily activities.

2. De-stress. (This is a big one.) To that end, make a list of your daily activities and tasks that cause you stress. Divide the list into two parts: one comprised of unavoidable, necessary tasks; and the other detailing the noncritical, self-imposed activities. Edit out as many of those self-imposed stressful tasks as possible and free up your schedule for relaxing, spontaneous, stare-into-space time.

3. Organize your home and work space, putting things into an order that works for you. Cleaning closets, rearranging bookshelves, and reducing clutter are ways to make your life and spirit feel refreshed.

4. Focus on personal hygiene: get rid of old clothing and expired makeup, treat yourself to a professional haircut, and use fragrance and herbal infusions to refresh yourself!

5. Go to the gynecologist, dentist, and internist at least once a year for a "well-woman checkup." Preventing illness is a lot easier and less costly than trying to deal with it after the fact.

6. Meet with a psychologist. Sharing your journey and opening your soul to a compassionate listener is important

you time—you need the outlet to blow off steam and learn new coping skills. Defy the negative stigma associated with mental health and think of it as beneficial and essential . . . which it is.

7. Exercise your body as well as your mind.

8. Spend time with a friend regularly.

9. Remember that hope floats—throw it out on your sea of wishes and dreams and see what happens.

Caring for Yourself Benefits Everyone

When you can imagine possibilities that may bring about successful change in your life, you're building your resiliency muscles (which is the kind of workout everyone can benefit from). Remember that being resilient is a characteristic that will help you power through the difficult times in life. When you can change your mind-set from thinking that everything is hopeless and impossible to one where you can see hope and possibilities, you're acting like a resilient person. Here, you're working from an inner locus of control, which means you *believe* that your actions can and will affect the course of your life.

One of my daughters recently went through a crisis that required her to refocus her thinking and reach deep into herself for strength and courage. Even though it was a difficult personal challenge for her, her inner will to thrive persevered, and she came through her crisis with an amazingly clear vision for her life. She developed a new creative outlet that has great potential, and she and her husband are raising their two young children with a newfound sense of strength and faith. The reason she was able to face her difficulties with such bravery is because she took the time to focus on her own well-being—time she hadn't previously allowed herself.

And just so you don't fall into the trap of assuming that you're not allowed to spend too much time caring about (and for) yourself, I'd like to remind you of something. It's been proven over and over again that when you take the steps to make your life better, the people around you benefit significantly as well. So if you need to get your personal celebration regimen started by telling yourself that your own care is not just about you, go ahead. Please be aware, however, that it actually *is* about you.

Celebrating yourself is in fact like going to church, a mosque, or temple. You are a unique and special individual who deserves to "let your little light shine." In order to keep the glow on, however, you'll need to adopt healthy habits and life-coping skills. One of the most important habits you can develop is the ability to make peace with your past so that you can continue to move forward. Dragging around emotional baggage that hurts or encumbers you is a total waste of time, energy, and effort. Give yourself credit for the things you've done well and your accomplishments, and forgive yourself for your transgressions, whether perceived or actual. Shit happens . . . God understands.

If celebrating your very being still poses challenges for you, learn to cultivate compassion for yourself; acknowledge that you've made mistakes along the way, but then strive to put your personal saga into proper context. I've mentioned this before, and it will come up again and again as a valuable intervention and exercise: *put pen to paper.* Studies have shown that people who can write positive stories about incidents in their lives are happier and healthier in their old age.

Be thankful for who you are as a woman, and give yourself permission to be proud. Admit that you have value, validity, and worth; and let your actions and demeanor show those around you that womanhood is as precious a state of being as manhood. Here's how:

- Be an example of strength to the women and girls around you.

- Learn from your past and then move on.

- Think of yourself as wonderful—represent your equality as a human being in the way you hold your body, the way you express yourself, and the activities that you pursue.

- Make a concerted effort to change the zeitgeist of the 21st century for the better by telling your unique female story in your own voice.

Walk the Walk

Helping humanity move toward this higher level of being is clearly a challenge. To meet it, you must hold yourself accountable—you'll need to do more than talk about it or merely agree that a change needs to come. You'll also need to be the first to "walk the walk."

We're struggling with mind-sets here. Just like the male mind-set, our female mind-set has been stewing for centuries

. . . making for a complicated brew. It takes courage, passion, patience, willingness, and determination; along with the intricate fusing of unique, divergent flavors or perspectives to change mind-sets. A difficult task for sure. But hey, what could be more important?

Women are chronically suspended in that murky area between tradition and progress: we wish to go forward, but we struggle with the expectations of the culture we were raised in. Don't let the murk cloud your vision. Have a serious discussion with your "interior-behavior editor." Establish your belief in yourself, set positive actions in motion to propel yourself onward, and engage in the celebration of your very *self*.

More than anything else I've learned thus far, the realization of my own personal power, my innate worth, and an appreciation of myself is what keeps me grounded. At the same time, this realization allows me to fly. Such a flight is an exhilarating experience. In case you don't recognize the feeling, breathe it in . . . it's called *freedom.*

Personal Tasks

● Write about your experiences, make amends by expressing your feelings (if only to yourself), and then let it go. Tear up what you've written, and make peace.

● Resolve to tell yourself happy stories about your life—reframe incidents by putting on rose-colored glasses if you have to, but just put a positive spin on them. It'll make a big difference.

- Banish the negative thoughts you're harboring and change your mind-set into one that imagines positive possibilities going forward, rather than sinking into the sadness or disappointments of the past.

- Decide what coping skills you'd benefit from, and then make an effort to learn them. For example, esteem building, anger management, stress reduction, assertiveness, positive visualizations, and meditation are wonderful skills to master.

- Describe five of your passions, and determine to spend more time engaging in them.

- Decide upon five things that you can do to feel better about yourself and your life today.

Wisdom from Your Peers

"Women are invaluable, the backbone of family and society. We work inside and outside of the home. We make a living and then come home to help our children (our future) with their homework, make dinner, support our husbands, and so on. We volunteer in the community and at our children's schools. Multitasking is our way of existence, and our work is never done. Without us, society would fall apart. Women are to be respected and held in the highest regard."
— **Julia A.,** United Kingdom

"I think that as part of the maturing process, everyone has to learn how worthwhile they are. There will be times in all our lives when we feel unworthy—a lack of self-esteem is the cause of many of youth's problems today. The trick is to have belief that we've tried our best and that failure at something does not mean that we will always fail; we can learn from that experience."
— **Florence S.**, entrepreneur, Malaysia

"My own life has been extraordinarily diverse. I grew up in a traditional Chinese family in Hong Kong as the lowest person on the totem pole: a second daughter who was quickly followed by three sons. My childhood was an all-too-familiar litany of abuse and neglect. If the common wisdom were true, I should have been a miserable failure in life, struggling to overcome a low sense of self-esteem and fighting a losing battle to win the affection of parents who were never going to give me the acknowledgment I craved. And yet I managed to rise through the executive ranks of the international-business world and become an influential corporate leader, speaker, consultant, author, and philanthropist . . . my life has proven that what I had was enough. Merely surviving in my family gave me the skills and the inner knowing that guided my career and my success in life. I built on those early traits through trial and error with the help of Spirit and many teachers as I journeyed through life."
— **Marilyn Tam;** writer, inspirational speaker; Hong Kong

"I gave birth to my first baby later in life. I'd put off starting a family so that I could establish my business and never really considered the consequences. After three miscarriages, I began to believe that maybe I didn't deserve to be a mother, since I selfishly put my career first over starting a family. My husband and I accepted the fact that it would probably be just the two of us forever. Imagine our surprise when we discovered that I was pregnant with a healthy baby boy at age 42! I realized that it had nothing to do with whether I was worthy of being a mother or not, and that I deserved this gift as much as anyone else. Thank God for miracles!"
— **Julie Ashton**, casting director, USA

"Have I always known I was worthwhile? I don't know— my experience is weird because I've always been in extreme conflict about that. I think that I believe myself to be worth- while, therefore I put huge expectations on myself for perfection. Then when I don't stack up to this ideal, which I very rarely do, I feel crushed and worthless. So I'm always in a battle with myself about that."
— **Tina Tyrell**, photographer, USA

"To be truly free and to grow in self-esteem, you can't give up your growth, pursuit of fulfillment, or happiness to anyone. Choose to treat yourself with dignity and proceed to move toward full love, wisdom, freedom, and joy, knowing that <u>you</u> are the authority over you."
— **Lilburn Barksdale**, USA

Journal Questions

- Do you accept and acknowledge yourself as you are?
- What do you do to show yourself that you care?
- Do you pay attention to the quality of your life?
- Have you stepped out of your routine lately to try something new and exciting? If not, why?

Self-Worth Affirmations

W.O.R.T.H.
Wisdom
My unique qualities define my individuality.

W.O.R.T.H.
Optimism
I am creative. I create happiness.

W.O.R.T.H.
Responsibility
I am taking charge of my future by being financially aware and prepared. My well-being is up to me.

W.O.R.T.H.
Tenacity
I am part of the solution. I advocate for positive change.

W.O.R.T.H.
Honesty
I know myself. My personal power emanates from self-awareness.

CHAPTER 12

Creating the Life You Want:
Living the Life You Create

"Take your life in your own hands and what happens?
A terrible thing: no one to blame."
— **Erica Jong**

Are you living the life you want, or do you secretly feel that you've "settled" for an existence that's giving you less than you deserve or isn't what you dreamed of? Regardless of modernity and whopping upgrades in the level of women's participation in the decision-making process of society, there are many among us who continue to be swept along with the tide of tradition, seemingly helpless (or just unwilling) to change culturally enmeshed habits and rituals. Maybe we're simply biding our time for the perfect opportunity to speak out, stand up, and take a leadership role in life.

If you have the sense that you're merely along for the ride, hitched to someone else's Prius while you wait for your turn—the turn that you're convinced someone of higher authority will undoubtedly give you—recognize that today is the day God made. Don't waste it.

Yes, patience is a virtue, and it does seem that all the saints in history had great big doses of it. But you must avoid making the mistake of using patience as a smoke screen for procrastination. Ask yourself the following:

- Are you currently pursuing any of your passions?

- Do you feel included, connected, and balanced in your world; or are you continually feeling rejected and detached?

- Are the tasks and jobs you do satisfying to you? If not, why do you continue to do them?

- What changes could you make that would make your life more fulfilling? Do you have the courage to make them?

- Do you accept life's challenges and try to surmount them, or do you feel overwhelmed by them to the point of giving up?

No matter what your circumstances are at this very moment, come to terms with the reality that *you play a part* in them. As difficult as it may seem, you have to make an effort to take an objective look at the conditions and results of your life. If you continually feel depressed and are sure that it's due to the state of your bank account, for instance, reevaluate your perspective. It's fairly clear that the quality of your life is *not* directly dependent upon your financial bottom line; it has more to do with your ability to function with the cards in your hand and your capacity for resiliency.

With that said, there's no reason why you shouldn't learn to be a better poker player—there's nothing wrong with figuring out how to use the cards you were dealt with more cunning. Once again, it comes down to personal responsibility and intentions. You're in charge of actualizing your dreams and goals, so take conscious actions to fulfill them. And realize that the *quality* of your life (that is, your satisfaction and overall contentment) has an impact on the *quantity* of your life as well.

For women, it's not enough just to create a satisfying life for ourselves—although I'll repeat once again the mantra that it *begins with us*. We've always been concerned with the better good of our communities, children, families, and fellow females. As connection-oriented and hardwired with a need to affiliate and nurture as we are, it's not surprising that even when we build psychological models to help other women, we're also considering the greater good of society at large. I'm referring to a basic precept of feminist psychology that suggests personal growth and healing should be accompanied by activism to bring about societal change.

While you have worth whether you're consciously aware of it or not, creating and actualizing the life you want to live requires effort and proaction on your part: your actions, intentions, and behaviors have a significant impact on how you *experience* your own worth . . . and ultimately on your quality of life, too.

Avoid Overgeneralization

Did you know that the pain of rejection nearly always stems from overgeneralization, or illogically deciding that one unpleasant thing that happened to you will happen over and over again? This repetition won't actually come to pass unless you *make* it—have you ever heard of a self-fulfilling prophecy?

Overgeneralizing is a waste of your precious time. It's also very important that you avoid going so far as to attach a negative label not only to a disappointing event, but to yourself as well. In the parlance of psychology, such a response would be a *cognitive distortion,* which is essentially the term used to describe a faulty thinking pattern.

Reframe your thoughts by sticking to what you know for sure. Encourage yourself with positive statements when life pitches you a curveball, and use the difficult lesson as an opportunity to grow. For example, try: "While management gave the promotion I wanted to someone else, I'm ready for it. I'm willing to be even more proactive to get the next one." Or: "Although I'm sensitive about financial issues, I don't need to take the blame every time my husband and I fight about money. We both share responsibility for our financial status, and I am an equal partner. I'm not a victim."

Changing the past is impossible—but acknowledging it and learning from it is not only possible, it's productive and healthy, and it moves you forward. Create the life you want by being your own gardener, producer, scriptwriter, director, and storyteller. The more attention you give to a belief, dream, or goal, the more energy it has. Your attention and intentions can establish positive *and* negative energy, so do your best to create the former.

Your intention to live a wonderful and fulfilling life includes activating your talents and passions, engendering your sense of possibility, establishing your independence, affirming your faith, and building on your strengths. You go, girl!

Be sure to:

- Be honest about your circumstances in life. Speak your truth, and "tell it like it is."

- Remember that an event is just an event. Don't make rules stating that just because something unpleasant happened once, it's destined to do so again.

- Create the life you want by visualizing your goals, and then take the appropriate positive steps toward achieving them.

Make Connections and Create Opportunities

Even though this is *your* story, you don't actually need to go it all alone. By nature, we women are social creatures, and these days more and more of us are reaching out to each other to form mutually beneficial social connections. Many of us have done so by forming or joining book clubs (there are both face-to-face and online versions), charitable giving groups, or playgroups if there are young children at home. Those of us who are business owners may connect with one another by joining the local Rotary Club or Chamber of Commerce.

Recent studies show that women are flocking to online social networks in droves to pursue business leads, to connect with colleagues, to stay in touch with extended family and friends, to market our wares, and to take a break from the responsibilities of kids and other demands on our time to enjoy interaction with like-minded adults. We're creating the lives we want by using any and all resources we can get our hands on.

If you haven't discovered these amazing Web-based networking forums as yet, venture online and check them out:

- ♥ www.Blogher.com
- ♥ www.Shespeaks.com
- ♥ www.wholewoman.com
- ♥ www.iVillage.com
- ♥ www.DivineCaroline.com
- ♥ www.girlfriendscafe.com
- ♥ www.womenentrepreneur.com

As you learn to take charge of your experience of a happy and fulfilling life, you'll realize that there's no shortage of useful tools in your personal toolbox, including opportunity—*you just need to look for them.* There *is* plenty of success to go around. Your happy life is not dependent upon everyone else's actions, although you'll obviously take notice of them. Be mindful that *your* experience of happiness begins *in your own mind.* You'll attain satisfying experiences by being proactive and determined, as well as by projecting the possibility and reality of their existence.

When you get the hang of turning off your mental filter—the one that tends to pick out the negative events to focus on—you'll be better able to perceive your experiences without attaching cognitive distortions to them. At this very moment, you're creating the life you want. Since you're an amazingly creative person, you should be using *all* the colors in your rainbow, whether you're in a group of kindred spirits or spending time alone:

— See things in all their colors, variations, and possibilities. Resist black-and-white, all-or-nothing thinking. See all sides.

— Realize that not all experiences are "a walk in the park." Obviously you're going to have pain and heartache sometimes, and there will be disappointments and regrets. But rather than building a rock-solid case for chronic, recurrent failure or establishing a set of rules based solely on your difficult experiences, use the hard knocks you encounter to grow stronger, happier, better, more in tune, more aware, and more at peace. There is a saying that "God won't put anything on your plate that you can't handle." Believe it.

— Don't discount or disqualify the positive experiences in your life. Take ownership of them!

— Gather the facts before you jump to a conclusion.

— Resist the urge to catastrophize your experiences; and watch that you don't minimize, exaggerate, or magnify the importance of things in your life. Although it can be a challenge, try to be objective.

— Be especially mindful of all the *musts, oughts, shoulds,* and *shouldn'ts* that you lay on yourself. Guilt is not a positive motivator—eventually it eats at you and makes you angry and defensive. Besides, in most cases you probably have nothing to be guilty about.

Advocate for Others . . . and Yourself

Careers and finances are major aspects of the life you create, but they don't just spontaneously occur; they require your magic touch. Fortunately, you and millions of your girlfriends have become extremely hands-on in this area. The latest trends show that rather than opting out of the workforce to raise families, more and more of you have opted back in—or, in actuality, you never truly opted out.

Two-career families are on the rise. While cost-of-living increases and a shaky economy are certainly contributors to this, such a boon in the workforce also reflects a tide change for women in general: we want to grow, we want to have our share, we want to be independent, and we want to thrive.

For many of us, pursuing and enjoying a vocation outside the home is a contributing factor to a satisfying life. We want to have positive, productive, fulfilling lives . . . and we're done waiting for someone else to provide them for us.

Unfortunately, there remains a significant gap between the demands of work and home, and this gap is most profound for women on the bottom and middle of the pay scale. This is especially true today—poor and middle-class families are entering the current recession in uncertain circumstances. A recent report from a major news source stated that although incomes of the middle fifth of families had increased 1.3 percent, the bottom fifth of families have *declined* by 2.5 percent since the 1990s.

Needless to say, our sisters in these economic strata frequently have meager resources for child care, and they don't tend to receive health care and retirement benefits. Clearly it's tougher for women with scant resources to create the lives they dream of. While it isn't impossible for them to beat the odds that are stacked against them and overcome their huge obstacles, they could certainly use a hand up. And this is where the power and input of women who have managed to bridge that gap becomes especially critical.

You and most of the women you know would probably say that you've been given ample opportunities to succeed, ample access to education, and ample support from family and friends. You might be able to state emphatically that you've never felt marginalized or restricted simply because you're a woman; you were raised to know that you have the potential to be happy, successful, and fulfilled in whatever domain in life you choose.

But the reality on the ground is that women in general are lagging behind in a multitude of important developmental and liberating thresholds in life. In some countries and cultures around the globe, females have scant options for gaining equal status. What can the rest of us do to help them increase their chances? We can become advocates.

Those of you who have found your own water level— you've succeeded in attaining an education and a career that supports your needs, and you have the energy and resources to spare and share—can be the agents of change. You can advocate for your fellow females who still struggle to accomplish those goals, helping them forge the essential link needed to build their own bridges. How? Try these suggestions, and then add some of your own:

- Share your knowledge, and trust your instincts.

- Create solutions for change for the women and girls around you who are struggling to achieve independence and fulfillment.

- Continue to think outside the box and challenge antiquated boundaries.

- Contribute to a fund that helps build capacity and teach women how to maximize their resources.

Feminist psychologists seek not only to heal the individual woman—to provide support and validity to a specific client's unique feelings and needs—but they're also seriously dedicated to pressing for the societal changes required to better include and represent women in the mainstream dialogue of life. In the end, this serves *all* of humanity.

Among its departments, the American Psychological Association includes Division 35, which is the Society for the Psychology of Women. This is an organizational base for feminists (both female *and* male) interested in the psychology of women. While members certainly encourage feminist research and education, they also advocate that women *take action* to sponsor new public policies that advance female standing and equality in the full scheme of life; actions that will ultimately engender social justice for all. Talk about *Mother Nature. . . .*

Trailblazing feminist psychoanalyst Karen Horney, who occupies a prominent place in the annals of psychology, wrote extensively about the importance of understanding female behavior and cognition. She focused on *current character structure*—a term she used to describe a system of mostly permanent motivational traits that determine how an individual relates to others and reacts to various stimuli, rather than delving overly much into the early development of that individual's personality. This focus continues to have significant influence on psychological theories today. However, Horney also emphasized how critical it is that all of us who are able to do so lobby to change the dysfunctional societal rules and ancient rituals that have shackled women to a lopsided female perspective in the first place.

Basically, your marching orders are to resolve to get your needs met and to live the life you imagine for yourself. This, in turn, will fire up your courage to join the public dialogue, which is an arena you need to become comfortable in—because the public forum is the one you'll need to join in order to pave better, safer, and more equitable roads for your daughters and other fellow females as well.

By the way, don't let the idea of going public with your opinions scare you. You may not want to join picket lines, run for office, or volunteer for a campaign, but you can make your feelings known by voting. You can also write letters to your local and national senators and representatives. Trust me, when you're passionate about your beliefs, it is energizing. You'll be amazed at how vocal you can be.

In addition:

— Stretch against perceived margins and restrictions that would infringe upon your ability to enjoy a bountiful, satisfying life by finding like thinkers. For example, join your city council, local school PTA board, or woman's fund.

— Make an effort to understand what feminist advocates have been lobbying for: banning violence against women, promoting parity in pay scales, affirming personal rights, prosecuting rapists, and the list goes on. Check out *Ms.* magazine, or visit their online version at **www.msmagazine. com**. Another source of information is **www.ifeminists.com**, and **www.apa.org/divisions/div35**. Make it your business to learn the *truth* about how the population of women are faring.

— Realize that a feminist perspective is one that embraces *equality* for all girls and women alongside boys and men. It's not about the denigration of our male counterparts, but rather the long-overdue *liberation* and celebration of the female.

— And you can't forget to advocate for yourself—if you don't, you may very well feel ignored and invisible; or worse, victimized and marginalized yourself.

One particularly unpleasant incident in my life brought this last lesson home to me. A man I once knew told me, and I quote, "You'll never be anything but a secretary." First of all, let it be known that *there is nothing wrong with being a secretary.* Most professionals today, regardless of gender, are totally indebted to their assistants and, to be frank, would be nearly lost without them. It was my profession for many years, and one that served me well.

However, at the time of the delivery of that snide remark (which wasn't meant as a compliment), it felt like a conviction of the crime of inadequacy. This guy wanted something from me that I was unwilling to give: *sex.* What a surprise. He didn't like being turned down, so he began to wave his macho "I'm smarter and more important than you are" flag. He tried to exert emotional pain to control me or punish me for refusing him.

His attempt worked for a time. I was psychologically wounded, as the owner of the mouth that delivered that comment had intended. Unfortunately, back then I had very low reserves of the self-esteem that would have helped me respond with a snappy "Fuck you and the horse you rode in on" kind of comeback. Consequently, I felt the sting of that statement in my heart for years. It was like a storm cloud that blocked out an otherwise bright and sunny day. But eventually, the sun began to shine for me again.

There is a place inside you that knows, indisputably, that you're an amazing individual with unlimited potential. When you let the opinions of others eclipse your own, it's easy to give in to criticism and put-downs. But when you allow your inner voice to talk back and ground yourself in the knowledge that you have a right to be here—that you have the ability to be your own person—you'll begin to advocate for yourself.

Once I started to become my own champion and took responsibility for standing up for myself and creating the life I wanted, I was no longer easy prey to such psychological warfare. Poof! Storm cloud gone. What's the lesson to be learned here? *Don't let another person have that much power over your emotions and state of being.* Seek out your inner counselor, and listen to what she says. You'll gain insight that will fortify you. For many of you, this will be a truly religious experience.

It can also help to:

- ♥ Learn to manage your emotions; establish your center and emotional anchor.

- ♥ Advocate for yourself by speaking *truth* to power.

- ♥ Fuel your own personal power source by maintaining a positive self-concept and inviolate sense of self-worth, despite what such energy vampires and happiness detractors may say to you.

It's Up to You

Ultimately, creating the life you want means that you'll need to come to terms with the fact that *nobody is coming to save you.* Regardless of what your parents did or did not do or others have done and have not done, you really *do* need to take charge. You can pretend you don't know this—you can continue to wait for a knight in shining armor to handle things—and you can live in denial about how much impact or lack of it you have. But you truly need to cut to the chase and accept the truth. When you talk to yourself honestly, you can make a pretty good assessment of how things are going for you.

If your life isn't playing out as smoothly or as successfully as you'd like, make changes. And although you can't expect someone else to resolve all your problems for you, you *can* reach for reinforcements. Seek out a good friend and confidant to share your troubles with, or identify a counselor or specialist who's knowledgeable in the area of life that's showing you a hard time and ask for advice. And then, armed with information and more confidence, face the challenge. When you do the work, you'll overcome your obstacles. The very act of telling your story honestly, of being authentic and true to yourself, is the foundation of the basic life design you want to create and joyously live.

Never discount your feelings and wishes and hopes and dreams. They're valid *and* valuable, so go after them. Your life—this one that you're conscious of—is the only one you've got. *Start using it before you lose it.* Since you can never turn back time, start creating the life you want right now by tuning in to how you're presently living.

Take a few minutes to read over the following questions:

1. What area of your life gives you the greatest sense of satisfaction?

   ♥ Family/partner
   ♥ Career/finances
   ♥ Achievements
   ♥ Recreation/avocation
   ♥ Charity/giving

2. Which areas of your life feel like they've fallen short of your hopes and dreams?

   ♥ Family/partner
   ♥ Career/finances
   ♥ Achievements
   ♥ Recreation/avocation
   ♥ Charity/giving

3. What stands in your way of appreciating the life
    you have and of creating more joy for yourself?

    ♥   Disappointment
    ♥   Regrets
    ♥   Control and abuse issues
    ♥   Helplessness
    ♥   Disbelief

4. How can you make changes that will make you
    feel happier about those areas of your life?

    ♥   Take positive action
    ♥   Take responsibility
    ♥   Have faith in yourself
    ♥   Seek professional help
    ♥   Reevaluate your goals

Now go back and do the following in your journal: make a list of your answers from items 1 and 2, answer question 3, and then apply your responses in question 4 to your previous answers.

Remember that there's value in the process. Keep your eye on the prize and know that your life is the actualization of your *own* exceptionally *worthwhile* game plan. And finally, take what you've got to deal with in the here-and-now and make it work for you.

Personal Tasks

♥ Strengthen your resolve and use your willpower. In order to enjoy fair and equal vocational advancement, you're going to need both.

♥ Be prepared to accept the challenge in front of you. Believe in your abilities.

♥ Make a personal choice to live a fulfilling life. Your authenticity is what helps build your self-worth and esteem.

♥ Be motivated. Creating a life for yourself that's satisfying and vital requires you to persevere even when the odds seem stacked against you. Be willing to learn your life lessons, difficult as they may be, so that you can grow.

Wisdom from Your Peers

"Since men have historically held most positions of power, a woman's perceived worth has been granted, so to speak, by the approval of a man (such as by the title of 'Mrs.'). This is still true, albeit to a lesser extent today than in yesteryears.
Men, however, have been victims of their own egocentric worldviews—now commonly portrayed as society-approved gender-role norms—in that they've denied the 'feminine' characteristics within them. I believe that the true worth of women will be recognized when men no longer feel the need to deny the parts of them that currently make them question

their manhood, and the question will become,
'What makes a <u>person</u> worthy?'"
— **Rima Mason**, USA

"As a child of the civil-rights era, my parents taught me
that I had worth as a person, which wasn't diminished
by gender or color. This is perhaps my greatest life lesson.
When I entered my profession, I was undaunted by the lack
of female role models. I had a positive attitude and worked
hard to excel because I knew I could. My hard work has
brought me many joys and rewards. Often I'm the first
black female architect people meet or hire. Many men have
asked me along my career path about my experience of the
'double whammy': being black and female in a white-male-
dominated profession. I never gave it much thought, certainly
not as much thought as they apparently had! I guess, upon
reflection, I find my circumstances both amazing
and powerful. I'm blessed to be a woman. And I'm
passing these lessons on to my children."
— **Karen Duncan Bonner**, USA

"I was good at sports, and when there were teams picked
in school, I was always chosen first. More important, I
always felt I was smart and nice . . . I believed that I would
always shine through. This is a perfect example of how we're
conditioned to think that our achievements define us."
— **Shelli A.;** mother, philanthropist; USA

"I'd tell the youth of today to respect a woman for her sexuality and femininity, and to accept these aspects of her as well as respecting her dignity, personal privacy, and freedom of choice."
— **Eva K.**, psychologist, Austria

"I want my son to know that women are to be valued as equal partners and appreciated for bringing a different but equally important skill set to the table as men do. As for my daughter, I want her to know that she can be anything she wants to be, that no profession or course of study should be off limits to her, and that her work in the same profession as a male should be equally compensated."
— **Gahl Burt**, volunteer, USA

Journal Questions

- What are you doing to create and live the life you want?
- Are you satisfied with the direction you're going? If not, what changes could you make?
- How can you strengthen your inner core?
- Could you be doing more to manage your expectations?

Self-Worth Affirmations

W.O.R.T.H.
Wisdom
I learn from my mistakes and use them
as an opportunity to grow.

W.O.R.T.H.
Optimism
I do whatever I choose to devote my intention to.
I act with confidence.

W.O.R.T.H.
Responsibility
I speak truth to power,
and I defy outdated stereotypes.

W.O.R.T.H.
Tenacity
I never give up on my dreams.
I set my goals, and I go after them.

W.O.R.T.H.
Honesty
I have found my voice, and I am
creating my own narrative.

CHAPTER 13

Mentoring the Future: Sharing What You Know

"Setting an example is not the main means of influencing others; it is the only means."
— **Albert Einstein**

Whether you personally feel the tug of self-worth issues or not—even if you are perfectly satisfied and fulfilled and are enjoying a safe, free, healthy, and financially secure life—be aware that your experience is not ubiquitous. Across the globe, millions of our sisters still struggle against a worldview that essentially amounts to a caste system relegating them to the lowest levels, which puts them at a disadvantage in multiple domains in life. In instances like this, the female sense of worth is on life support.

What can *you* do to help? The first step is to recognize that gender inequalities are endemic in certain societies: for example, child brides, female genital mutilation, sex trafficking, violence against women, and so forth. The next step is to raise awareness: speak out about and expose the lie, and defy the misuse of power.

Reflect on the following significant changes that have been made to rectify some disparities for females across the globe:

- Schools are being built for girls in rural Pakistan and Afghanistan where few existed before.

- Some communities that used to enforce female circumcision are beginning to advocate against it.

- Women have more access to career choices and power positions than ever before.

But having said that, more development for women is clearly needed. While you're reading this page, for example, women in developing nations are feeling the brunt of those disparities: 70 percent of the 1.5 billion people living on a dollar a day (or less) are female. Clearly, their immediate prospects are fragile and limited. We need to do something *now* if we're going to make a difference for them. How can we speed this process along?

A Call to Action

A critical component for change resides within your own daughters and the other young women you know. The way you express your own self-worth, as well as how you acknowledge it in others, will have immense impact.

With that in mind, what are the most important things you'd like your daughters and female relatives and friends to know about being a woman? I hope your list includes:

- Independence
- Responsibility
- Self-respect
- Marketable skills
- Economic stability
- Freedom
- Compassion
- Faith
- Parenting skills
- Creativity
- Ingenuity
- Equality
- Self-preservation
- Authority

The overview is that women have accomplished much and are steadily gaining access, voice, and power. Yet when we take a closer look, statistics covering the current status of women and children, especially girls, tell a different story that isn't so shiny and upbeat. Women are disproportionately plagued by violence; in fact, nearly 50 percent of all sexual assaults worldwide are perpetrated upon girls 15 years of age or younger. And approximately one-third of American women—31 percent—report being physically or sexually abused by a boyfriend or husband at some point in their lives. Experts think that this number is just the tip of the iceberg, however, since only a fraction of those women go to a shelter or report the abuse.

In domains that have been recognized as status changing, such as education, females still lag sadly behind. Despite the fact that every year of schooling increases individual wages for women (and men) by a worldwide average of 10 percent, of the 121 million primary-school-age children who aren't in school, 65 million are girls. And two-thirds of the world's 862 million illiterate are women. Although such a litany of statistics can be mind-numbing, force yourself to absorb them—for even in societies where women have easy access to higher education, the power of a woman's voice continues to be subdued, marginalized, restrained, or muffled.

How can you help them? Do you personally have a handle on the status-changing areas of *your* life? Have you found, and do you use, your voice? Have you developed a *heuristic,* a method or process that works for you, in order to seek a life that's harmonious and fulfilling? How will you share what you've learned with the young women around you to help them achieve the goals they've set out for themselves? In many cases, these goals can only take place when there's recourse against physical and sexual abusers; equal pay for equal work; an equitable balance of power; a louder, more significant voice in political dialogue; and a power seat in the corporate boardroom.

If this sounds like a call to action, you're getting my drift. *Act. Speak out. Mentor.* As women across the globe lay claim to more and more of a proper share of the goodness in life, it's vital that you concurrently teach new values to your young *and* to the young people with whom you interact. You're a torchbearer, a model, an example, and a significant and invaluable mentor for the future generation. So command respect and value yourself. Show—by your words and actions—that women and girls are equally vital, valuable, and capable. And share what you know with a young girl or boy: sponsor a child through Big Brothers Big Sisters or become a mentor for a kid in need.

When I was a youngster, my mom signed me up to be a Camp Fire girl. At the present time, the organization includes boys *and* girls and is called Camp Fire USA, but back then it was a service-oriented enrichment program for girls only. My membership in this club was a huge part of my young social life and generated some of my fondest memories. I got the chance to interact with other adult women besides my mom and aunts, and these women became role models for me.

I was taught how to appreciate nature and enjoy the great outdoors, but I also learned about the world I lived in. In age-appropriate ways, my fellow campers and I were taught to be safe and to be aware of our surroundings. I had the opportunity to go to day camp (and sleep-away camp once a year); I learned the value of giving to others, the importance of mutual respect, and the responsibility of community service at a very young age. I will never forget the nighttime campfires, roasting s'mores, and singing songs; nor will I forget caroling at the senior-citizens' home during the holidays or making small decorations for the meal trays for the local hospital. The camp counselors and group leaders were my mentors and heroes, and I remember them all with fondness.

Youth groups such as Camp Fire USA, Girl Scouts, and Boy Scouts are a benefit to society in numerous ways. They open up doors to places kids might not have the ability or perhaps even the imagination to go to. Such organizations can help build confidence and community spirit—something young people today need more than ever.

It's extremely important that you pay particular attention to the messages you give your sons about women. Resist the typical stereotypes of weakness; and teach strength, worth, ability, and power instead. The way you conduct yourself in all areas of your life sends a powerful message to those adorable little ones now filling hospital nurseries and preschools . . . those little sponges that will gobble up whatever society dishes out to them. You're a conduit for messages that will be good or bad; extreme or moderate; antiquated or contemporary; pliant or rigid; multidimensional or narrow-minded; misogynist, feminist, humanist, individualist, or collectivist; and on and on. Like it or not, *you are a role model.*

Research shows that parents have a propensity to encourage gender-appropriate activities in their young children. What does this mean exactly? It means you can present a *balanced* view of activities or a *narrow-minded* one. Pink or blue; doctor, scientist, builder, princess, teacher, nurse, secretary, firefighter, astronaut, or pilot—such gender-role attitudes (and, in fact, your expectations as a parent) have a direct link to your kids' conformity to such roles and ultimately to their self-esteem.

Please don't doubt that you and I have a hand in how kids grow up, how women are perceived as a gender, and how history is written. It's an intimidating task, this idea of mentoring the future . . . but don't shy away from it, since it is incredibly important.

Essentially, your words, behaviors, and actions are laying the architectural foundation for what the kids of today will do when they become the adults of tomorrow, whose business it will be to run the world. Will they run it in a way that's more respectful of women? When they're in charge, will females experience more freedom, more empowerment, and more equality? Or will they use their power positions to perpetuate fallacious stereotypes, antiquated cultural rituals, and gender bias? You'll need to begin this balanced education immediately, because studies show that kids demonstrate gender-stereotyped behavior and preferences by as early as 18 to 24 months of age. *Coochi-coochi-coo . . .*

Live Long and Prosper

As you can see, your responsibility to acknowledge and take ownership of your self-worth is much more than a personal healing exercise. It's a clarion call to help future generations understand the importance and legitimacy of their *own* self-worth and to view themselves as leaders, strategists, and stakeholders in the game of life. Fulfilling this responsibility will mean taking your multitasking propensity to another level. In actuality, you and the generations of women that follow will be taking on *even more* responsibilities than you currently have.

As you grapple with mentoring the future, most of you will also be caring for your parents, who make up an increasingly aging population. With advances in technology and health care, we're quickly heading into a world where we'll have 70-year-olds taking care of their 90-year-old parents, with the overwhelming majority of them being women. I'll fit into this group, since I'm only 21 years older than my eldest daughter. That eventuality portends to be a *humbling* experience, I'm sure. But we can all be prepared for our future by taking responsibility for it.

As a cohort that may live longer than our predecessors, though possibly with more chronic illness, our generation needs our youthful leaders to take note and begin to plan for this eventuality. Are the youth of today prepared for this responsibility? In a word, no. Their parents aren't truly ready either, although we're taking on the task in droves.

A survey taken by the AARP in 2004 stated that as many as 44 million Americans—21 percent of the population—currently care for an adult family member or friend. And now that approximately 78 million baby boomers are approaching retirement age, these numbers will increase. The current economy makes this multigenerational living situation even more difficult.

It's ironic that in many ways our health-care system has both helped and hindered us. Although many lives are prolonged via research and new drugs and treatments, the health-care system falls short of addressing chronic illness that often comes with aging. Today's health care doesn't come close to addressing the fourth quarter of life—along with global and national security concerns, this will be one of the most salient topics to be discussed for the foreseeable future. Be part of this dialogue, since, one way or another, health care and the lack of it affects you and your family.

Be sure to prepare for a long and healthy life by:

- Buying medical insurance and keeping it updated
- Setting up a retirement account in your 20s and letting it grow
- Being aware that you may need to help care for your aging parents
- Understanding that you may need your children to help care for you

Impact and Influence

Thanks to our sheer numbers alone, it shouldn't be difficult for women to have a major impact on society:

our gender makes up approximately 50 percent of the population and the workforce. Yet our influence in society, and our impact on the rules that regulate societal behaviors and habits, hasn't reached the levels one would expect from such a sizable group. As of 2007, nearly 84 percent of the members of the United States Congress are still men, 82 percent of U.S. governors are men, and 90 percent of top-clout positions in business—those that wield the most power—are held by men.

For all the hyperbole about advancement in human rights, equal rights, and overall superiority, the sad reality is that the United States ranks 67th internationally in women's political leadership—behind Afghanistan and Cuba. How is that possible? It's the result of a persistent and strong resistance to change, along with a deeply rooted schema of what women are *supposed* to do, think, and be. Remember that the world still generally believes that *masculinity is synonymous with authority.* And the underlying and enormously strong cultural ideal for females in America remains enmeshed in outdated puritan, censorious Protestant values that tend to view us as wives, mothers, helpmates, and nurturers.

While I'm on the soapbox, I need to reiterate that I'm not suggesting that those roles be abandoned. Not even close. We usually handle such roles expertly and are uniquely geared for them—but being a wife and mother is only a part of our female story, and it needn't prevent us from engaging in a plethora of *other* roles and endeavors.

With that fact clearly evident to so many of us, it's imperative that we express, expose, and teach a multi-dimensional perspective of "woman" to our kids as well. In order to help persuade the zeitgeist of the future to become more female friendly, we must use our formidable voices to make more female-centric choices.

Let's try the following:

— Validate all females' ability to live the life they want. Let's encourage fearlessness, personal responsibility, integrity, and ambition.

— Teach girls to be powerful and to accept and respect their own authority. Let's support them in their endeavors to participate in all domains of life—including sports, politics, science, art, mathematics, business, medicine, education, and religion—and acknowledge their *ability* to do so.

— Promote a positive perspective of women and girls that applauds and encourages curiosity, intelligence, assertiveness, and growth. Let's state clearly that there is no arena in life that women should be barred from. Many of us with exceptional strength and grit have already proven that we can fly in outer space, compete in sports, and head governments. Girls and women can and should participate at every level, and not merely as observers or helpmates, but as leaders and strategists.

— Educate boys to respect women as equals—let's teach them that females are *not* to be viewed as underlings to be dominated or subjugated in any way. We must disallow the concept of "women as objects" or "women as the weaker sex." There is *nothing* weak about a woman's sex.

As constituents of the female gender, our work is cut out for us. To bring about the kind of change necessary to fulfill the United Nations' Millennium Development Goals (which I mentioned earlier in the book), we must inject *our* opinions into mainstream thought in the earliest stages of a child's education process . . . as infants. And then we need to back up *our* resolve collectively in whatever ways we can to bring about the changes *we* collectively seek.

We must:

- Encourage girls to study political science in school.
- Teach boys and girls that women are strong, intelligent leaders.
- Get involved in politics (if we have the desire) and run for office.
- Make it our business to know the political machinations of our community.
- Support other women in their efforts to achieve their goals.

Political Empowerment

One of the ways you can promote a more balanced, harmonious, and worthwhile social and global agenda is by electing other women into political office. Lots of them. Can you imagine the kind of dialogue that would take place in the political arena if women were equally represented? Can't you just hear the conversations? There would be a lot more consensus building, a lot more teamwork, and a lot more attention paid to *holistic* endeavors.

With more power seats by virtue of sheer numbers, we should be able to dissuade gender, racial, and stereotypical slurs—such as labeling strong women "manipulative and controlling bitches." What's up with that? When we have equal participation, perhaps our female candidates won't continually be subjected to sarcastic, derogatory, diminishing shout-outs like, "Hey lady, cook my dinner and iron my shirts."

The sad truth is that the objectification of women is so pervasive in our society that decorum and respect are often easily tossed aside. In fact, although this is no excuse, many people who perpetuate such gross lapses in judgment and respect don't even realize their behavior is abhorrent. In 1984 when Geraldine Ferraro was running for vice president, for instance, a columnist for *The Denver Post* wrote: "Ferraro has nicer legs than any previous vice presidential candidate." Did anyone write about George Bush's thighs? I don't think so.

While we all like to get the occasional compliment, bear in mind that Ms. Ferraro was a *vice presidential candidate* in one of the most esteemed nations on the planet. The mouthpiece was supposedly a respected journalist in the mass media, which has access to millions if not billions of individuals. On the face of it, do you suppose that this comment was a compliment, or was it actually meant to belittle Ms. Ferraro?

It seems that the media has little problem printing opinions about a woman's legs and her cleavage, but have they ever been overly concerned with whether our male candidates are "right" or "left" dressed? Nope. (Incidentally, these terms refer to which pant-leg side a man prefers to arrange his "junk" on.)

Here are three things you can do to show your dissatisfaction when women are trivialized and marginalized:

1. Write letters to newspapers to voice your discontent over the opinions of journalists who use gender slurs.

2. Show your disapproval of policies, laws, and the perpetuation of stereotypes by writing blogs, sending e-mails and letters to your local and national lawmakers, and responding to newspaper editorials with opinions of your own.

3. Stand up for women who dedicate themselves to public service. Whether you agree with their policies or not, at the very least they deserve respect and a chance to voice their opinions.

Why some individuals feel emboldened to disrespect women candidates is beyond me. However, when society (including the media) permits a derogatory focus on the superficial and stereotypical of our gender, we denigrate strong, viable, incredibly intelligent females; and we relegate them to comic relief for the oh-so-powerful and not-to-be-messed-with dominate culture of *man*.

When we focus on the superficial—such as hairstyle, clothing designer, lipstick choice, cleavage, and ankle size—authority can be quickly eroded. News flash? This is *not* funny, productive, or what we want. When we can claim a more balanced representation of women in political office, we'll be able to bring about a significant behavioral change in the way women are represented in general.

You can help bring this about, and here's how:

— Vote in *every* election. Make it your business to learn what's at stake and what's being proposed each time a vote comes up. Read the fine print. How will your choice affect women and families? How will it affect you personally?

— Be an example to the girls in your life: Study politics. Be interested in business. Encourage discussions about global issues. Resist and dismantle stereotypes.

— Participate in civic activities and teach your young about social responsibility. Volunteer, and advocate for the greater good. Show your daughters and sons that peaceful change is possible, but not necessarily spontaneous. It requires effort and proaction. Encourage them to be the solution.

Paying It Forward

As you establish your own self-worth on solid ground, do what you can to encourage women and girls around you to embrace *their* abilities, self-worth, and validity. At the same time, be aware that millions of your sisters will need more than encouragement.

An experience that made this message poignantly clear to me occurred not long ago at a family shelter in the San Fernando Valley. I was among several volunteers serving lunch cafeteria-style to the 30 or so residents in a temporary-housing shelter. One woman in particular caught my attention, as she and her three young boys sat quietly at a table in the corner. The strawberry-blond-haired boys ate their lunches in silence, while their mom just stared down at her lunch tray. The redheaded woman had pale, freckled skin like her sons; and despite the fact that she was wearing sunglasses, I could see red blotches at the corners of her eyes—a telltale sign that she'd been crying. The image of this little family in desperate circumstances made my heart jump into my throat. I couldn't help but wonder what had transpired in this woman's life to make her essentially homeless with three young boys to care for.

Single mothers are particularly vulnerable. I still get tears in my eyes when I think of this one because I realize that could have been me. There was a time when I was living paycheck to paycheck, and any number of circumstances could have put me in a similar, desperate position. Even now, I'm particularly sensitive to the plight of single mothers who receive little or no spousal support, and for whom economic solvency is but a dream.

You may have had a similar experience—so if you have the means, do something to help. Be part of the international, global dialogue that seeks to level the playing field for women. Do your part to help give your fellow females a chance to participate fairly, and to do so with the *respect* they deserve. Join a woman's giving fund and put resources into the hands of those who need it most. As you surely know by now, women are the best bet. Give them tools to help them raise themselves up, and not only will they climb higher, but they'll bring everyone else with them as well. And encourage participation by girls in the political management of your school, community, city, state, and country.

You can be confident that what you do today to mentor the future will go far in helping to make your "senior moments" more enjoyable. And since you can't stop time (among other things), you know that those moments are just around the corner. Make sure that, at the very least, they're fulfilling ones.

Personal Tasks

♥ Be cognizant of women's ways of knowing. There are several ways we capture and absorb our knowledge: via what others show and tell us, via our subjective view of what we see, and the cultural societal *groupthink*. Young girls still glean their information in all of these ways.

♥ Note all of the voices *you're* privy to. Your own inner voice and your quest for "self" is subjective knowledge; procedural knowledge is the voice of reason; and integrated voices from all directions comprise our constructed knowledge. Knowing *how* you know is an art form.

♥ Understand the roadblocks young women of today still face—such as gender bias, restrictions to corporate advancement, and limited access to the financial and business decision-making process—and help dismantle them.

♥ If you're in a position to do so, hire women and girls.

♥ Resist objectification by others, along with *self-objectification*, which essentially means that you see yourself through others' eyes. Teach girls that just like their male counterparts, they can master their environment. Female bodies are not projects that need to be constantly refitted merely for male consumption.

- ❤ Be a positive influence. Use your voice, your abilities, and your unique position in life to persuade growth and development in others—particularly in young girls and boys. And this includes engendering a compassionate moral compass. Moral education is essentially the conditioning of the heart and mind; so, in your own way, be a teacher.

- ❤ Open your eyes. If you've grown up in relative calm, prosperity, and security, be aware that not all women and girls are assured of such circumstances. Learn about what females world-wide are facing—for example, the *dalits* in India, formerly known as "the untouchables"—and ask yourself who will speak for them.

- ❤ Understand that by raising your own awareness, you'll be better able to transfer that mindfulness to the girls and boys in your life. In significant ways, you'll be improving possibilities for them while at the same time supporting the growth and development of women outside of your community.

Wisdom from Your Peers

"When I was in high school, I worked as a teacher's assistant in a Hebrew school. There was one girl in particular who was very bright and sweet, but she was uneasy in her skin and didn't really fit in. I spent a little extra time with her, just

talking about 'girl stuff,' such as fitting in, boys, self-respect
. . . whatever was going on in the mind of this (then) ten-
year-old. We stayed in touch through the occasional phone
call, but I didn't see her again for several years. I heard that
she formed a good group of friends in junior high, graduated
from high school at the top of her class, and had a wonderful
school experience in general. I later learned that she wrote a
paper in high school naming me as a person who had been
a significant influence in her life. It made me realize that I
could make a real difference—that just a little bit of time and
attention could have a significant impact on someone's life."
— **Judy Friedman,** attorney, California

"I would tell the youth of today this: You are not alone in this
world. Surround yourself with people you respect and care
about. Reach out to others, strive to be the best you can be,
support others along the way, never burn a bridge, and be
the kind of friend you want to be yourself. Remember that
you can have it all. Remember, too, that there are always
people less fortunate than you. You can make a difference
by your actions, thoughts, words, and deeds."
— **Claudia Looney,** hospital fund-raising, California

"It's important for our daughters and sons to be able to see
women and men as different but equally valued members of
society. The measure of a person's worth has nothing to do
with gender and everything to do with character. Each of us,
whether man or woman, should have an equal opportunity to

express our worth as an individual. Women as a group bring different qualities and gifts to the table, but whether those gifts are manifested in the service of good is a choice each woman has to make for herself."
— **Terry Rosenberg,** New Jersey

"Having a sense of self-worth may be more difficult than being seen as worthy by others—many of us judge ourselves more harshly than we do others. For me, my worth is very much bound up with extending myself to others, practicing compassion, and trying (but not always succeeding) to make a contribution to our shared life here and now."
— **Jacquelyn McCroskey,** professor and advocate, Texas

"I'd say that a woman's worth is not defined by whom she's dating or sleeping with or by who's in love with her. I think a lot of women stay in relationships that aren't necessarily the right ones because it's easier than facing the idea of being alone. But it's important for women of all ages to understand that we're not defined by whom we're with. It's important to understand and feel comfortable with ourselves first as individuals, and only then can we be open to truly worthwhile relationships."
— **Lauren T.,** sous-chef, California

"I was born during World War II to an unwed mother. We became refugees and lost everything to the Russian occupation. The war interrupted my education, and my mother died of cancer when I was 18. I was not dealt a great hand—but in spite of that, I feel that I have and hold a 'royal flush' of blessings and accomplishments."
— **Erika Brunson,** interior designer, East Prussia

Journal Questions

- What are you doing to help future generations?
- How can you make a difference for at least one child today?
- Did you vote in the last election? If not, why?
- Did anyone in your life stand out as a mentor or role model? What can you do to emulate her?

Self-Worth Affirmations

W.O.R.T.H.
Wisdom
I am part of the solution!

W.O.R.T.H.
Optimism
I set a positive example to those around me.

W.O.R.T.H.
Responsibility
I am responsible for the life I create,
and I therefore make it better.

W.O.R.T.H.
Tenacity
I grow stronger from adversity. The goals I work
harder for are those that bring me the most pleasure.

W.O.R.T.H.
Honesty
My worth comes from within me.
I have a right to be here.

CHAPTER 14

Giving Back: Recognizing Your Truth and Passing It On

"Never, never, never quit!"
— **Winston Churchill**

You've made it through a multitude of personal inquiries; thought about pointed questions; spent some time soul-searching; and hopefully have rediscovered, and are happily emanating, your self-worth. Congratulations! Now you've come to one of the most pivotal chapters not only in this book, but also in your life: putting what you know to work for the benefit of others.

Since this is a book about a woman's self-worth, I'd be remiss if I didn't repeat that one of the most important things you can do to make a difference for future generations is to become an advocate for female causes. As I've noted throughout these pages, when you help women, the aid they receive trickles down to their children, their families, and their communities. Women who have the opportunity and resources to help themselves will share the bounty and change their environments for the better. It's a proven fact that women *create* the village!

While self-worth is something that germinates inside *you,* you feel it most strongly when you experience equilibrium in your universe. I'd love to tell you that self-worth is a constant feeling; a ready, steady horse in your stable. Although it *should* be, clearly the ups and downs of life can have an impact on your sense of self-worth, even if only temporarily. Women who are faced with more than their share of life's inequities—thanks to the whims of hormones, politics, war, cultural rituals, family strife, ill health, disabilities, or some other uncontrollable force—are more prone to *disequilibrium.* This is obviously not the state of being you and your fellow planet mates strive for.

So do what you can to support projects that foster welfare and education for girls as well as for boys, and also to see that a fair share of the world's resources are directed to women. And be the ambassador of solutions, keeping in mind that nobody promised it would be easy. Females face numerous obstructions in the quest for equality, parity, and voice; these formidable roadblocks won't be dismantled without significant effort. Nevertheless, this is not a pursuit you want to give up on . . . too many are suffering. Finally, *be the change you seek.* This is a simple concept, and one that each one of us can follow.

The Joys of Giving

Did you know that giving to others is good for your overall health and well-being? It's true! *Giving of yourself to help the greater good has the added benefit of enhancing your own sense of self-worth.* Research by the Points of Light Institute revealed that when troubled juveniles were instructed to do community service by helping younger children read and finish their homework, an amazing transformation occurred: troubled kids who volunteered their time to help others ended up skipping school less, avoiding many risky behaviors, and becoming more considerate of other people.

Most of the teenagers in the Points of Light Institute study stated that they got a happy charge out of helping other boys and girls. It turns out that their selfless actions gave them a sense of worth, and for some of these young people, it was the first time they'd *ever* felt it. The kids began to feel a sense of *responsibility* to the little ones they were helping. The simple act of devoting some of their time to the welfare of their community instilled in them a sense of belonging to it. *Aha!*

So if you have troubled teens in your own life, get them involved in a community-service project—preferably one that serves other youngsters—such as a teen hotline, peer-to-peer tutoring, or after-school sports or activities. You may see a beautiful transformation.

And if *you* are feeling down or undervalued, give of your time to a homeless shelter, children's hospital, senior-citizen's home, or free health clinic. You'll quickly discover how good your life really is, how much you have to offer, and how valid and worthwhile you *truly* are.

As you can see, *giving back* has multiple meanings and isn't all about money. You may think of such action as charity, philanthropy, altruism, or having a social conscience. Yet when you first come in contact with the word *philanthropy,* you may think it's something that only people with lots of time and money on their hands are associated with. Perhaps you attach it to well-to-do "ladies who lunch," thinking that it all sounds very highbrow.

Just to be clear, however, according to the dictionary, *philanthropy* refers to "the desire to promote the welfare of others"—and if you can do that and eat lunch at the same time, then more power to you. All of us can be philanthropists, regardless of age, ethnic group, or economic status. It's neither highbrow nor about giving handouts; it's about community.

While philanthropy is often expressed by a significant monetary donation to worthy causes, writing a check is only *one* way to flex your giving muscles. Many of you already use a combination of resources including time, treasure, and talent to support causes you care about. Without blinking an eye, I bet that you volunteer at your kids' schools, participate in clothing drives for disaster victims, send donations to support abused women, run marathons for cancer, and chair fund-raisers for worthy organizations. The common goal of all givers is to *promote the welfare of others.*

Giving back isn't just something to do when you have extra time and money—it helps complete the circle of life that you're in. Incidentally, giving back includes sharing your truth or narrative; you bear witness to what you see and experience in your life so that those who come after you will have a road map to follow. You're an important piece of the puzzle of life . . . please don't forget that.

These three suggestions should help activate the philanthropic, altruistic side of you:

1. Turn your helplessness into helpfulness. Even if your life circumstances are difficult, you'll benefit from volunteering your time and resources to someone less privileged than yourself. Take a lesson from the people who attend AA meetings: by helping each other, they help themselves. When you give to someone else, you discover gratitude and, as they say, *serenity.* Whether you're packing groceries for a food bank, reading to grammar-school children, volunteering at a free clinic, being a Big Sister to a disadvantaged girl, writing letters for senior citizens, or donating personal-hygiene products to a woman's shelter, you're making a difference in someone else's life.

2. Seek release from greed and want and focus your attention on the bigger picture. Poverty, hunger, violence, and environmental decay are all serious global issues that could bring our civilization down. Here in the United States, as in most developed countries, there's often an illusion that there are plenty of goods and services to go around, but don't be fooled by the excesses of a few. Many are struggling to get their fair share of life's booty, and women and children (particularly girls) often end up on the bottom end of the pecking order, even when it comes to getting their basic needs met—including water, food, and sanitary products. So pick a cause and make it one of your life's purposes. Your own self-worth will be enhanced when one of your passions, goals, and/or purposes in life includes making the world we live in a better, more hospitable place.

3. Recognize that you have special gifts and talents, and use them to help make someone else's life better. In case you don't think that you *have* any special gifts or talents, just take a moment to consider those things that come naturally to you and seem to produce amazing results. Your talent, by the way, could be an easy smile, your intuition, the capability of being compassionate, a love of teaching, or the ability to listen

. . . there are a host of options, so use your imagination. If you can't yet identify all of your fabulous gifts and talents, simply practice random acts of kindness.

An Ethic of Service

Do you think that everyone should be obligated to do something to give back, or is it a choice? Some people are obviously more charitable minded than others: certain individuals have plenty to share and decline to do so, while others have virtually nothing yet give of themselves anyway. Perhaps compassion and caring are latent traits that become active when our environment requires it. Some respected neurological scientists suggest that due to unique brain chemistry, women feel especially compelled to help others; we're apparently hardwired to serve.

Is there a certain time in life when you should start giving back to society? Is it a social construct or modeled behavior? Are altruism and charitable behavior introduced to you as a child and therefore dependent upon your upbringing?

Several noted psychologists refer to *stages* in life and the fulfillment of certain requirements to describe human behaviors. Abraham Maslow's well-known hierarchy of needs, which I mentioned in Chapter 6, posits that you're *motivated* by those needs instinctively; however, you must meet certain criteria in one stage before going on to the next.

In Maslow's hierarchy, it's only after most of your personal survival needs are met that you're able to pay attention to esteem and self-actualization needs, which include your contributions to a better society. And according to psychologist

Erik Erikson's stages of psychosocial development, it's in middle adulthood—or some point between the ages of 35 to 65—that individuals feel a compelling need to give back, and they derive true gratification and meaning from participating in charitable activities.

While the chronology of meeting certain survival needs before others is essentially the same for everyone, I'd bet that for most of you (like me), a sense of community empathy and charity was initially forged during childhood. You can pay this positive behavior forward by:

- Teaching your own children to share
- Cultivating caring and compassionate behaviors
- Making teamwork and a sense of gratitude an everyday occurrence in your family

My parents instilled an ethic of service in me and my siblings from the very beginning. They volunteered at our local church and grammar school; and as kids, my brother and sister and I were enlisted in canned-food drives and car washes to raise money for community projects. My mom had the foresight to take us kids to the municipal pool for lessons, and it turned out that I was like a little fish in water. I earned my junior-lifeguard badge as soon as possible, and then I volunteered to be part of the group of instructors who would train to teach swimming lessons to disabled kids.

As I mentioned previously, my experiences as a Camp Fire girl had begun to instill in me the sense of responsibility to give back to our community—but the truth is, I was having a heck of a good time. The social-consciousness component was a by-product rather than the goal of my participation, at least when I was young. Still, it's well known that kids benefit substantially from the camaraderie and community-building skills that service clubs and volunteer opportunities encourage, and I thank these experiences for engendering in me a passion for community service that endures today.

At that young stage in my life when I was a Camp Fire girl and swimming instructor (I was also a candy striper), I didn't associate the concept of service and giving with monetary value—it was more *intrinsic* than that. At any rate, our family didn't have any extra money to give away, so that sort of gift wasn't even an option. But "elbow grease," as my dad called it, was something we had *plenty* of. Over the years my siblings and I learned that our actions, time, and participation were beneficial to others; and just as important, they were our *responsibility* to our community.

We were taught to count our blessings. We had a home, clothes to wear, food to eat, and parents who loved us. Even though we didn't have a lot, we were still ahead of the game. The subtext of the lesson we were learning behind our community involvement was not only that it would *feel good* when we did something kind and caring, but also that working together for the common good was the *natural* thing to do. My mom's mantra was, "It's better to give than to receive." My dad's was, "If everyone pitches in, the job will get done."

To that end:

- Teach your children to be cognizant of others' hardships and struggles.

- Give gently used clothing to homeless shelters, and participate in food drives for your local food bank.

- Sponsor a woman and/or child from a developing nation, and engage your children in the process.

- Instill a giving, sharing mind-set to your young children. Begin modeling this behavior early, and forge a lifelong sense of compassion.

- When it's age appropriate, encourage community service in your kids. Most schools have lists of local agencies and nonprofit organizations that would be happy to have your family's participation.

- It's important that you recognize there are stages of life, but you must also realize that helping others can be a part of *every* stage. Try engaging your kids in a socially conscious club or group from a young age; choose to give back to society, and raise your children to follow your lead.

One Starfish at a Time

While you probably recognize that acts of charity and community service are good and necessary, you might not believe that *you* personally can make an impact on society. You may feel overwhelmed with the enormity of need that exists: statistics that speak about poverty, hunger, gender inequalities, HIV and AIDS, infant mortality, war, genocide, an environment at risk, and a persistent preference for boys over girls in India and China—two of the most populous countries on Earth—can take your breath away and make you feel woefully impotent. You're only one person after all, and there is so much to be done.

But don't be discouraged. *Begin.*

As they say, "If you save one person, you save a community." I once heard a story that exemplifies this concept, and it goes something like this:

> One day a little girl and her grandfather were walking along the seashore. It was low tide, and spread out on the sand for as far as they could see were starfish, stranded out of water and dying in the heat. Every few steps, the little girl bent down and picked one up and threw it back into the sea. The little girl and her grandfather walked along this way for a while in silence, while she continued to bend down, pick up a starfish, and toss it into the water.
>
> Finally, the grandfather said, "What are you doing, Mary? You can't possibly save them all."
>
> The little girl bent down and picked up another starfish, tossed it in the ocean, and looked up at him resolutely. "But I saved that one, Grandpa."

Yes, the need is great, and perhaps at this moment you already have your hands full. But my advice to you is this: don't allow questions about your expertise or availability—or even the fact that you're only *one* person—stop you from getting involved. *If you make a difference for one person, you can manifest a world of change.* I'm betting that as a woman, albeit one who's very busy, you haven't yet reached full capacity.

There's no limit to how much you can love, and basically, that's what this is all about: *unconditional love.* Besides, it's precisely when you have too much on your plate that you'll be encouraged to learn how to juggle—or in the vernacular of women today, *multitask.*

Here's how to get started:

- Pick a cause you care about and get involved: send a check, volunteer your time, or offer your expertise. Pass out magazines to patients in a hospital, take food to senior shut-ins, recycle your gently worn clothing to a homeless shelter, or the like.

- Avoid judgment. Remember the saying "There but for the grace of God go I," and heed it. Be grateful for your blessings, and help others navigate their difficulties. It's not up to you to judge.

- Give unconditional love.

You Can Help Others . . . and Change the World

If your life has been filled with disappointments, tragedy, abuse, or violence, you might not think that you "owe" this world much. On the other hand, you may have realized that if someone had given you a hand when you needed it, you would have surmounted your difficulties that much sooner. Many of the women who responded to my questionnaire about worth stated that they feel especially gratified when they're helping somebody else.

When your philosophy of life is set to a moral compass that instills in you the wish to "do unto others as you would have them do unto you," such activities will add to your overall sense of authenticity and make you more conducive to *experiencing* happiness. Funny how that happens. Researchers who study happiness and quality-of-life issues have amassed plenty of data that support the act of giving as a significant life-enhancing ingredient. Everybody wins . . . you know the feeling.

Make it a habit to give of your time, talent, or treasure; because there is no shortage of ways you can impact society and effect positive change. The critical question is not what you'll do, but rather, how quickly can you begin?

Peruse the following list of options; if something resonates for you, please visit the Website in parentheses, where applicable:

- Volunteer at a school, library, or senior-citizens' retirement home (**www.volunteermatch.org**).

- Join Big Brothers Big Sisters and mentor a child (**www.bbbs.org**).

- Become a foster parent (**www.fosterparents.com**).

- Donate blood or volunteer at a children's hospital.

- Donate food to a local food bank, or go online to help end world hunger by giving funds to Share Our Strength (**www.strength.org**).

- Donate to a global organization like Heifer International to help communities build economic independence (**www.heifer.org**).

- Donate clothing and other necessities to a homeless shelter or domestic-abuse safe house.

- Sign up to help build a house with Habitat for Humanity (**www.habitat.org**).

- Help fund the mission of Doctors Without Borders (**www.doctorswithoutborders.org**).

- Participate in a sponsored walk or run a marathon for a cause you believe in, such as cancer research (**www.cancerschmancer.org**).

- Sponsor a child through global organizations such as Plan International (**www.planusa.org**), Save the Children (**www.savethechildren.org**), Mercy Corps (**www.mercycorps.org**), and UNICEF (**www.unicef.org**).

- Join the board of a nonprofit organization that focuses on a critical need in your community.

- Marshal your resources and chair a fund-raiser.

- Give to an organization that provides microloans to women in developing countries, such as Grameen Bank (**www.grameenfoundation.org**) and Kiva (**www.kiva.org**).

- Advocate for women and girls by joining and donating to a woman's fund, such as the Women's Funding Network (**www.wfnet.org**) or Women for Women International (**www. womenforwomen.org**).

- Buy makeup from Peacekeeper Cause-Metics. The profits of certain items are donated to women who live on less than one dollar a day, and for them, it's pennies from heaven (**www.iamapeacekeeper.com**).

- Write a check—be it a big one or a little one, all will be welcomed.

These suggestions are obviously like a grain of sand in a huge dune—there are countless more. But hopefully they'll provoke a thought process that will reveal an area or cause you could see yourself connecting with. Please do.

If you're still on the fence, keep in mind that confronting deadly challenges is the status quo for millions of women in war-torn countries. Yet even though there are sadly too many examples of tragedy, there are also lots of stories of strength and bravery.

One notable example occurred in the country of Liberia, which is a totally different nation now than it was 20 years ago—its transformation bears witness to what can happen when women take a stand to bring about change. During the bloody civil war that consumed the country beginning in 1989, women and children were targets of horrendous torture and violence. They felt helpless to stop the atrocities and unspeakable brutality perpetrated on them, their children, and other civilians. But despite their horror and grievous loss (and in the face of constant danger), some of these women banded together to forge the Liberian women's peace movement, persevering over several years in *nonviolent* efforts to convince the warring leaders to engage in peace talks.

The courageous women of Liberia faced imprisonment, torture, and death; yet they were determined to survive, and they wanted their communities to thrive. Although the price was steep, they gave tirelessly of themselves to steer their country on a more peaceful course, and eventually prevailed. Their activism and courage opened the door for Liberian women to enter the political arena, and it's primarily due to their valiant efforts that Ellen Johnson Sirleaf was elected as president of that country in 2005—thus becoming Africa's first female head of state.

The truth is, freedom isn't *free*. What you're enjoying today was fought for and earned by the efforts of your predecessors from every nationality, ethnicity, and economic group from all over the world. But you'll also be a part of a new dawn for the next generation. There may be times when the burden seems too heavy, your patience wears thin, or you lose your way . . . but never stop trying to make positive changes. Your struggle to redeem and improve society is *not* against the shade of your skin, the language you speak, or the country and culture you were born into. Rather, it's a struggle to speak your truth, own your power, change mind-sets, express your self-worth, and create the better world we all want our kids to grow up in. You must take *personal responsibility* to be the change you seek.

We can't lean too heavily on others to do the job—it will take the efforts of each and every one of us to ensure our growth as a civilization.

Whether you've reaped rewards from life or feel that you've been denied them, be one of those resilient individuals who help others simply because it feels right, just, and satisfying to do so. The following will help you on that path:

— Be informed. Investigate the dire circumstances that millions of women and children around the globe face.

— Make it your business to know the United Nations' Millennium Goals, which are to:

- ♥ Eradicate extreme poverty and hunger
- ♥ Achieve universal primary education
- ♥ Promote gender equality and empower women
- ♥ Reduce child mortality
- ♥ Improve maternal health
- ♥ Combat HIV/AIDS, malaria, and other diseases
- ♥ Ensure environmental sustainability
- ♥ Develop a global partnership for development

— Become familiar with the language of international law as it relates to women exposed to violent conflict. Be aware of the intent of the UN's Convention on the Elimination of All Forms of Discrimination against Women (CEDAW), and decide to help bring about change. As of 2008, CEDAW falls under the jurisdiction of the high commissioner for human rights in Geneva. You can go to CEDAW's Website: **www.un.org/womenwatch,** or to the site of the Office of the United Nations High Commissioner for Human Rights: **www2.ohchr.org.**

— No matter what, get involved. Start small at first and stay close to home until you find your stride, but be willing to jump into the big picture soon by helping out on a global scale.

— Join any of the internationally recognized groups mentioned in this book.

Find Your Balance

Before you dive into the charity pool and go full throttle, find your own rhythm—your own peace—and establish a safe harbor for yourself. After all, when you feel strong and secure in your own skin, you'll have more impact as a mentor and a leader. It's normal to want to feel important and be affirmed by others, but when you're in the act of selfless giving, haughty behavior and inflated views of yourself or your cause are uncalled for, so check *that* attitude at the door.

How can you help others without inadvertently abusing power? Diffuse the power struggle by engaging mutual respect. Here are a few suggestions:

1. Ask questions, and be willing to listen.

2. Collaborate.

3. Resist the urge to make comparisons and swift judgments.

4. If you want to help a disadvantaged population, ask for its input and discover what its needs are. Don't assume that you know all the answers for other people, because you could have it all wrong. For example, you might make a judgment call that education should be the first priority when in reality the community lacks available safe drinking water, sanitation facilities, or food. Ask the community leaders and help them resolve their problems, rather than assuming that you have all the solutions.

When your goals of helping and making a difference are clearly stated and not tied to a self-serving agenda, you'll be able to provide your expertise with grace and understanding.

In all aspects of your life, *including* philanthropy, seek an equitable power balance. Strive for harmony and learn to be wise. All around you are amazing mentors: thousands of women speak to you from history and urge you to succeed, to participate, to own your worth, to express your power, and then to teach the next generation how to take the baton.

Women can be incredibly strong and determined individuals, so be mindful of what your female predecessors have accomplished. When you read about the monumental efforts they exerted, not just for your rights but for all of humanity, you'll be inspired and—most important—*motivated* to continue their work. People can move mountains when they're provided with the right tools.

Know that your sense of self-worth is in part defined by the efforts you expend for the good of others. Giving back ensures that you confer something of yourself to posterity:

you're bestowing a gift to those you're serving, a memory to guide future generations.

Regardless of whether you feed one starving child or save an entire village, your philanthropy—your random acts of kindness, charity, and advocacy—will leave a mark. The message you leave behind states clearly: "I have self-worth, and I believe you do, too. We're part of a community; and in the end, we're all worthy, worthwhile, and valid."

Such conviction and clarity of purpose is what self-worth is all about.

Personal Tasks

- Document best practices, and then share them with others. Don't imagine that you need to re-invent the charitable wheel. There may be many organizations in place that are doing the work you wish to do, so work *with* them.

- Seek information from the community you wish to serve. The people will tell you if their most critical need is education, health care, safe water, agriculture, or sanitation—listen to them.

- You're not alone on this planet, and the culture you grew up in is not the preeminent leader or master race. Be mindful of other cultures, religions, and ethnicities. Our differences needn't keep us apart; they should engage us to learn more about each other. Develop multicultural awareness.

- Become an advocate. If you have the means, visit your senators and congressional representatives and make your opinions known. Your financial influence can have an impact in the political arena and help you bring attention to the causes you care about.

- Think globally, since international engagement is now a way of life. You can communicate with someone on the other side of the planet with a click of the SEND button on your computer or mobile phone—you may be able to *help* someone that far away just as fast.

Wisdom from Your Peers

"Do I consider myself a worthy woman? No, but I'm con-stantly striving to achieve this emotional fulfillment. There are 'takers' and 'givers'—I get my joy from giving. I don't think that I'll ever see myself as a worthy woman, but I'll always continue to give as long as it brings someone else joy."
— **Sigal Kremer,** marketing entrepreneur, Israel

"Making a choice to arrest my addictions and the patterns of my ancestors, along with the courage to confront the imprints of my parents and grow from them, have been the largest growth spurts of my life."
— **Jamie Lee Curtis;**
mother, actor, writer, activist; California

*"I feel my own worth every weekend when my husband
and our kids are all together in bed. I feel at peace and
complete love when I see what a wonderful family I have—
knowing that a happy family doesn't just happen.
That's when I know my worth."*
— **Jennifer Flavin Stallone,** actress and
business entrepreneur, California

*"Although I find the question of definition of worth
very subjective and think that it's all relative, I do think
that on a very base level, what defines one's worth is
honesty, honesty, honesty. In how we give and how we
share. It's about <u>quality</u>, not necessarily <u>quantity</u>."*
— **Morleigh E.;** mother, dancer, advocate;
California and Ireland

*"Women's worth is unique, and the way our brains seem
to be wired is the proof. I'd like youth and society to embrace
our strengths and acknowledge the physiological
differences that make us women."*
— **Victoria G.,** educator, Illinois

"As a young teacher I worked in an after-school program—Upward Bound. This program worked with inner-city high school students and helped them achieve their dreams of attending college. Many of these students honestly thought that this dream was unattainable: they had babies, or their parents were drug addicts or in jail. Upward Bound changed the lives of many of the students as well as my own. I brought home students and even had one or two live with my husband and me when their family situation became untenable."

— **Susan Dolgen,** philanthropist, New York

Journal Questions

- ♥ How are you paying it forward?
- ♥ What can you do to instill a give-back mentality in your children?
- ♥ What could you do today, tomorrow, and next week to make an impact on your community?
- ♥ How do you ensure that your children feel validated and have a sense of their own self-worth?

Self-Worth Affirmations

W.O.R.T.H.
Wisdom
I make a difference. I am capable!

W.O.R.T.H.
Optimism
I see the potential in others.
I provide solutions.

W.O.R.T.H.
Responsibility
I express gratitude for all that I have in life.

W.O.R.T.H.
Tenacity
I have unique qualities and passions that
make a difference in the world.

W.O.R.T.H.
Honesty
I refrain from judging others.
Instead, I help build bridges.

271

AFTERWORD

What I Know

The process of writing this book has taken me on a two-year romp of an adventure that evoked several new revelations for me—not all of which were painless or pretty. I want you to know that despite all I have learned and experienced regarding women's worth and our capacity for greatness, I understand *quite viscerally* that the road we must travel to expose, express, and own these feelings of innate worth can be littered with potholes. Maintaining a strong center can be more challenging than I care to admit. Although I totally get that there's more than one mountain to climb or issue to overcome, the strong, indefatigable center of who we are is always there in the end—ready to be revealed.

I put myself through the same exercises I posed to you as I was writing this book; I admit that there were times, because of events occurring around me, that I wondered how I could *ever* follow my own advice. Bear in mind that I acknowledge I'm coming from a position of entitlement. First of all, I'm living in the United States, where most of our freedoms are guaranteed . . . or, at the very least, are taken for granted. I enjoy good health, which on its own endows me with a leg up. I'm the mother of four and the grandmother of four, my octogenarian parents live with me, and I enjoy a happy relationship with them all. I have a vocation that I'm passionate about, and I'm successful at it. And finally, to wrap a bow around my basket of blessings, I'm happily, passionately married to an extremely successful man who credits me with part of his success.

With such a litany of luck, you might assume that I can't possibly understand the true underbelly of woe that exists for millions of women worldwide. But please don't jump to that conclusion. Life still pitches me challenges that can bring me to my knees. How is that possible? With such bounty at my fingertips, surely I should be able to withstand any blow, right?

So am I weak? Am I soft? Do I hide my strength? No. Or perhaps, yes—at times. Despite all I have, all I've been through, and all I know, I still have days when I struggle with self-doubt and concern about my ability to make everyone in my sphere happy. I still worry about my capacity to do the *right* thing as far as *they* are concerned. And, I must confess, I still come up against the worry that perhaps I don't deserve all that I have.

Heavy emotions, right? Not exactly what you wanted to hear from someone telling you to acknowledge your self-worth. I'm thinking that I'm not going to get a lot of sympathy, nor do I expect any. This is all part of the process. I've been blessed with riches beyond my wildest imagination—and I know that there are millions of women who, because of fate, are barely scratching out a living for themselves and their children on less than a dollar a day.

But just as you've probably discovered, simply because a woman lacks the necessities with which to sustain her livelihood, it doesn't necessarily follow that she also lacks self-worth. Conversely, we can't deduce that a woman who has every material possession at her disposal has the magic key; that she has discovered and is able to express her self-worth at all times, in all circumstances.

Our sense of worth—our compass for correctness, happiness, and personal power—is relative to each one of us. It's personal and subjective. It isn't connected to our material possessions. It isn't accumulated or accrued by our achievements, the people we know, the family we're born into, or the husbands we marry. It's more intrinsic than that, which is why every one of us, regardless of worldly circumstances, can claim it. The factors from which we each derive our sense of worth may vary, but the feeling that emanates as a result of recognizing our worth can be understood by us all.

Still, while we can *intellectually* grasp that our feelings, perspectives, and expectations can be self-driven, the realities we experience in our everyday lives may suggest a different story. Life is a challenge: It's not easy or even possible to be all things to all people. It's not easy or always possible to assert our power. Under certain circumstances, it may not be easy to *acknowledge* our worth and validity, let alone *assert* it.

Perhaps the ease with which we accomplish a thing is relative to other experiences we've had, or maybe we simply need to expand our ability to imagine. At any rate, just so you know that I have *not* been perched on top of a cupcake with only sweetness and delight all around me, I asked myself some of the same pointed questions I posed to you, and then I wrote stream-of-thought answers to them, just as I hope you have done. I'd like to share some of my personal introspections here.

1. What are you afraid of?

I'm scared shitless that my shortcomings and mistakes have irreparably hurt or negatively affected my daughters and son. I'm concerned that I'm too habitual; a perfectionist who has virtually no wiggle room; a control freak. I'm afraid that I seek approval too much and lack true grit. I'm afraid that I'm not good enough, that mistakes I made when I was a teenager and a young adult are coming back to haunt me now. I worry that I made too many stupid choices and took too many wrong turns in the road. I'm afraid that with all I know, I don't know enough. I'm afraid that even though I think I'm basically okay, sometimes I'm not worthy.

2. Are these fears based on reality? In other words, do you feel that you did something or behaved in some way to substantiate your feelings of fear and inadequacy?

No, my fears are not *all* based on reality. But I know that I did *plenty* of things when I was a young adult and young mother that contributed to my feelings of guilt and inadequacy. I got married at an early age, way before I had a clue about what I wanted to do with my life. I got divorced from my first husband and remarried someone whom I *knew* I didn't love. I worry that my two eldest daughters felt frightened, helpless, and perhaps even abandoned in their new surroundings, while I attempted to launch a career. It took me three marriages to finally get it "right." Am I just a slow learner? I sometimes think my "life illiteracy" compromised my children's well-being, fostering a recalcitrant fear of failure and a shaky sense of self-worth.

3. What can you do now to reframe your past experiences—to revise your distorted thoughts?

Ah, well . . . I suppose I could look at some of those experiences from a different perspective. The difficult incidents and circumstances I encountered in my life—such as failed relationships, lack of resources, and divorce—actually taught me valuable lessons. I learned to find my own courage and to speak my own truth. I learned that I could change my perspective, and that with personal effort, I could change my life. The self-assurance and self-esteem I gained from living through the fire of difficult times eventually made me available, both in mind and spirit, to love myself and then love another. Such personal knowledge made me attractive to a man with whom I'm now sharing the rest of my life. My fairy-tale dream actually did come true.

And although I regret any sadness or discomfort the course of my life caused my children, I'm comforted by the knowledge that despite my occasional misguided life choices, they're thriving. We're bonded together with love, compassion, and mutual respect. They're strong, unique individuals who understand that lessons will be forthcoming in life, and they're willing to learn them. I'm immensely proud of them; as I watch them grow, I feel a burgeoning sense of fulfillment, joy, and—yes—an increased sense of self-worth that I played a small part in that.

These are only a few of the answers I wrote in my own journal pages, but you get my drift. Our discovery of self-worth, and our ability to express and project it, are not static concepts. Change is the only constant in life, yet it's clear that we can set our inner guidance systems to be proactive. We can accommodate and adapt to change in ways that enhance our sense of well-being and increase our feelings of self-worth. In a phrase, *it's all up to us.*

Thank you for sharing this journey with me. I especially thank you for your willingness to open up your heart to your inner voice and to allow your *true* self to speak. I hope that your own life path is offering up many happy discoveries along your way, and that it will provide multiple interesting doors to walk through. I pray that your passage won't be too arduous, but when it is the toughest, you'll find inspiration from God and from *within* to continue on your way.

Know that I appreciate your worth as a woman, and I treasure the contributions you're making to future generations. As you know, each of us can do our part, and each offering is to be honored. When you bought this book, you helped make a difference for someone who's less fortunate than you are (I'm contributing all of my author's profits to women's funds around the world).

Thank you for sharing your self-worth with those around you. It's an extraordinary gift.

One Last Thought

Okay, humor me here. Being of the computer-connected information-superhighway generation, you've no doubt received many inspirational messages from friends and colleagues, and nine times out of ten, you probably just hit the DELETE key. But this one is a keeper. The author is unknown, but I'll speak for all of us when I extend a collective "thank you" for the thought.

> By the time the Lord made woman, He was into his sixth day of working overtime. An angel appeared and asked, "Why are you spending so much time on this one?" And the Lord answered, "Have you seen my spec sheet on her? She has to be completely washable but not plastic; have over 200 movable parts, all replaceable; be able to run on Diet Coke and leftovers; have a lap that can hold four children at a time; have a kiss that can cure anything from a scraped knee to a broken heart—and she has to do everything with only two hands."
>
> The angel was astounded at the requirements. "Only two hands?! No way! And that's just on the standard model? That's too much work for one day. Wait until tomorrow to finish."
>
> "But I won't," the Lord protested. "I'm so close to finishing this creation that's so close to my own heart . . . she already heals herself when she's sick, and she can work 18-hour days." The angel moved closer and touched the woman. "But you've made her so soft, Lord."
>
> "She _is_ soft," the Lord agreed, "but I've also made her tough. You have no idea what she can endure or accomplish."
>
> "Will she be able to think?" asked the angel.
>
> The Lord replied, "Not only will she be able to think, but she'll be able to reason and negotiate, too."

The angel then noticed something, and reaching out, touched the woman's cheek. "Oops, it looks like you have a leak in this model. I told you that you were trying to put too much into this one."

"That's not a leak," the Lord corrected. "That's a tear."

"What's a tear for?" the angel asked.

The Lord said, "The tear is her way of expressing her joy, her sorrow, her pain, her disappointment, her love, her loneliness, her grief, and her pride."

The angel was impressed. "You are a genius, Lord. You thought of everything! Woman is truly amazing."

"Yes, she is . . . and all women will be. All women will have strengths that amaze men. They'll bear hardships and carry burdens; but they'll hold happiness, love, and joy. They'll smile when they want to scream. They'll sing when they want to cry. They'll cry when they're happy and laugh when they're nervous. They'll fight for what they believe in. They'll stand up to injustice. They won't take no for an answer when they believe that there's a better solution. They'll go without so their family can have. They'll go to the doctor with a frightened friend. They'll love unconditionally. They'll cry when their children excel and cheer when their friends get awards. They'll be happy when they hear about a birth or a wedding. Their hearts will break when a friend dies. They'll grieve at the loss of a family member, yet they'll be strong when they think there's no strength left. They'll know that a hug and a kiss can heal a broken heart.

"Women will come in all shapes, sizes, and colors. They'll drive, fly, walk, or run to loved ones to show

how much they care. Their hearts will make the world keep turning. They'll bring joy, hope, and love. They'll have compassion and ideals. They'll give moral support to their family and friends. Women will have vital things to say and everything to give.

"However, if there's one tiny flaw in women, it's that they will often forget their worth."

SUPPLEMENT: Personal Journal Questions and Affirmations

You may have already pondered your responses to the following questions as you read this book. Perhaps you even followed my gentle prodding and began to write in your personal journal, using these questions as fodder to fuel your investigation. If you have, bravo. The information you've gathered about yourself may reveal secrets about "the who of you" that will inspire positive actions going forward. It can also be beneficial to read through these questions again. Would you alter any of your responses now that you've spent some time appreciating your *self*?

If you *haven't* found the time to devote to this journaling process yet, may I remind you that there's no time like the present? Read through the following questions, and allow them to inspire deep thoughts about yourself. I invite you to have a great one-on-one conversation with your *inner* you.

Journal Questions

1. What specific attribute, characteristic, or "fact" about yourself gives you a feeling of worth?

2. How can you make yourself feel better today?

3. What do you do to make sure you honor the work you do in your home?

4. What makes you laugh, smile, and feel joy? What are you doing to make sure that you experience those sensations every day of your life?

5. What steps can you take to ensure that you can express yourself with confidence?

6. What's holding you back from achieving your goals?

7. How is fear keeping you from moving forward?

8. What are you afraid of? Your husband? Your father? Your teacher? Authority in general? How can you overcome these fears?

9. Do you let people in your life make you feel worthless? Do you give up your own power? What can you do to stop that?

10. Do you always follow the crowd?

11. Do you feel confident enough to take the initiative to be different? How do you express this confidence?

12. What creative urges do you acknowledge and act upon?

13. Do you spend time creating? Do you allow yourself the freedom to design and explore?

14. When was the last time you took a walk outside, alone?

15. Do you view life as an optimist? If not, why is that? What's stopping you from seeing your glass as half full?

16. How can you become more assertive in your life?

17. Do you feel resilient? Do you bounce back from life's difficulties? If not, what would make you feel more secure and confident?

18. Do you surround yourself with people who are supportive of your goals and ambitions? If not, why is that?

19. Do you enjoy sex?

20. What do you like most about your relationship?

21. What steps can you take today to make your love/ sex life more enjoyable for you and your partner?

22. Do you have a reciprocal relationship? Do you feel that your intimacy needs are being met? If not, what can you do to change that?

23. Do you feel fulfilled in your marriage?

24. If you've gone through a divorce, have you fully recovered your sense of self-worth?

25. Do you harbor feelings of failure in your marriage?

26. What can you do to recharge the passion of your relationship?

27. How can you continue to grow as a person?

28. Does being a mother add to your sense of self-worth? Do you feel fulfilled in your role as a mom?

29. Did your parenting skills evolve naturally? What would you do differently?

30. Does your spouse/partner take an active role in the parenting of your children? If not, why?

31. Are you prepared to allow your kids to differentiate away from you? What can you do to get ready for that transition?

32. What compensation do you receive for the work you do at home? Is it equitable? If not, what would you change?

33. Are you dependent upon others for your livelihood? What can you do to buck up your own financial security?

34. Are you comfortable with the salary you're receiving? If not, when will you ask for a raise?

35. What can you do to feel more in control of your finances?

36. Are you a happy person? If not, why?

37. Does your happiness depend on the actions of others?

38. Do you spend much of your time *organizing* happiness for others in your life? What can you do to ensure your own happiness?

39. Do you accept and acknowledge yourself as you are?

40. What do you do to show yourself that you care?

41. Do you pay attention to the quality of your life?

42. Have you stepped out of your routine lately to try something new and exciting? If not, why?

43. What are you doing to create and live the life you want?

44. Are you satisfied with the direction you're going? If not, what changes could you make?

45. How can you strengthen your inner core?

46. Could you be doing more to manage your expectations?

47. What are you doing to help future generations?

48. How can you make a difference for at least one child today?

49. Did you vote in the last election? If not, why?

50. Did anyone in your life stand out as a mentor or role model? What can you do to emulate her?

51. How are you paying it forward?

52. What can you do to instill a give-back mentality in your children?

53. What could you do today, tomorrow, and next week to make an impact on your community?

54. How do you ensure that your children feel validated and have a sense of their own self-worth?

Affirmations

Finally, mark this page so that you can revisit it often. Make it a habit to start your day with a positive message to your soul. Know for certain, with every breath you take, that you *are* a woman who recognizes her self-worth.

Please read the following affirmations, and then *say them out loud:*

- ❤ I am confident.
- ❤ I am kind.
- ❤ I am well.
- ❤ I am healthy.
- ❤ I am attractive.
- ❤ I am intelligent.
- ❤ I am secure.
- ❤ I love.
- ❤ I am serene.
- ❤ I am calm.
- ❤ I am loving.
- ❤ I am happy.
- ❤ I am compassionate.
- ❤ I am radiant.
- ❤ I am careful.
- ❤ I am caring.
- ❤ I am safe.
- ❤ I am ambitious.
- ❤ I am independent.
- ❤ I am courageous.
- ❤ I am brave.
- ❤ I am creative.

- ❤ I am spiritual.
- ❤ I am precious.
- ❤ I am honest.
- ❤ I am strong.
- ❤ I am thoughtful.
- ❤ I am empathetic.
- ❤ I am altruistic.
- ❤ I am charitable.
- ❤ I am unique.
- ❤ I am honest.
- ❤ I am a survivor.
- ❤ I am grateful.
- ❤ I am free.
- ❤ I learn.
- ❤ I listen.
- ❤ I am determined.
- ❤ I am special.
- ❤ I am accomplished.
- ❤ I am a role model.
- ❤ I am priceless.
- ❤ I am woman.
- ❤ I am worth it.

ACKNOWLEDGMENTS

There is no way I could have written this book without the generosity of spirit and unwavering support of many incredible individuals. My husband, my parents, and my children offered steadfast encouragement throughout the writing process (although at times I'm sure they grew weary of seeing me stationed in front of my computer). I am grateful *every day* for their love and affirmation.

Thank you to the hundreds of women from near and far who took the time to respond to my questionnaire. Your thoughtful answers and personal stories are a strong, powerfully beautiful reflection of where women stand today, as well as how we'll ensure a happy tomorrow for future generations.

I extend a *special* thank you to some women in particular who went out of their way to make sure that this book is in your hands right now. To Jillian Manus, literary agent extraordinaire, I am forever grateful for your vision and your constant, indefatigable belief that I had a message worth writing. To Joy Noe, my deepest thanks for all you do for me. You are an extraordinary woman, friend, and assistant who brings a new meaning to the concept of multitasking. To Marilyn Flynn, Ph.D., dean and professor in the School of Social Work at the University of Southern California; and Jacquelyn McCroskey, also of the USC School of Social Work; thank you for sharing your perspective and encouragement.

To Dr. Ernie Katz, thank you for being my mentor and for showing me the depth of compassion that's required in a children's hospital. To my very special girlfriend posse, you are all precious beyond words. I thank you for sharing your insight for this book and for being the kind of angel friends I cannot imagine living without.

I've collaborated with some incredible women *and* men throughout this project, all of whom are seeking to make a difference in the lives of women and, by extension, their children and families as well. Thank you to Christine Grumm and Karen Brightly of the Women's Funding Network, for helping to facilitate my association with women's funds and for dedicating your formidable global resources to the needs of women. Thank you to Jody Weiss of Peacekeeper Cause-Metics, for creating a cosmetic company that not only is friendly to the planet, but that also donates the profits on certain items to women who live on less than a dollar a day. Thank you to Ahuma Adodoadji of Plan USA, for being the guiding light for a multitude of special projects across the globe that focus on women and children. Thank you to Pamela Stone of Heifer International, for spearheading so many national and international projects that uplift the lives of women, children, and men by giving them the tools they need to help grow their own economies; and thank you to Zainab Salbi, CEO of Women to Women International, for speaking your truth and for helping so many marginalized women in Iraq and beyond speak theirs.

The risk of thanking people individually is that I may fail to recognize all the others I've spoken to and queried. I've been mightily blessed with many girlfriends *and* male friends who have added richness to my life and ultimately contributed to the content of this book. I thank you all for who you are, and for your ability to see who I am, too.

SELF-HELP RESOURCES

A *What is Your Self-Worth?* personal journal ($9.95 retail value) that encapsulates and personalizes the tasks and quizzes that appear throughout the book—a road map, if you will, for each woman's journey—is available for free download (with purchase of the book) at: **www. whatisyourselfworth.com**. To obtain your free journal, enter the retail code: **735396784**.

As previously mentioned in the book, here are some Websites you may find useful:

- ♥ Women's Funding Network: **www.wfnet.org**
- ♥ PeaceKeeper Cause-Metics: **www.iamapeacekeeper.com**
- ♥ Plan USA: **www.planusa.org**
- ♥ Mercy Corps: **www.mercycorp.org**
- ♥ Kiva: **www.kiva.org**
- ♥ Heifer International: **www.heifer.org**
- ♥ Women for Women International: **www.womenforwomen.org**
- ♥ Grameen Foundation: **www.grameenfoundation.org**
- ♥ CARE: **www.care.org**

ABOUT THE AUTHOR

Cheryl Saban, Ph.D., writes extensively about women, children, and social issues. Using her background in psychology, she devotes a great deal of attention to philanthropic endeavors that focus on pediatric health and research, education, relationships, and the empowerment of women. In addition to *What Is Your Self-Worth?* she has written *New Mother's Survival Guide, Recipe for a Good Marriage, Recipe for Good Parenting,* and several other works. She currently lives in Los Angeles, California, with her husband, two of their four children (when they're not away at college), and her octogenarian parents. She receives regular doses of love and attention from her four grandchildren.

Websites: **www.whatisyourselfworth.com** and **www.cherylsaban.com**

NOTES

NOTES

NOTES

NOTES

Hay House Titles of Related Interest

YOU CAN HEAL YOUR LIFE, the movie, starring Louise L. Hay & Friends
(available as a 1-DVD program and an expanded 2-DVD set)
Watch the trailer at: **www.LouiseHayMovie.com**

THE SHIFT, the movie, starring Dr. Wayne W. Dyer
(available as a 1-DVD program and an expanded 2-DVD set)
Watch the trailer at: **www.DyerMovie.com**

❧ ❧ ❧

THE AGE OF MIRACLES: Embracing the New Midlife,
by Marianne Williamson

*THE ART OF EXTREME SELF-CARE: Transform Your Life One
Month at a Time,* by Cheryl Richardson

EMPOWERING WOMEN: Every Woman's Guide to Successful Living,
by Louise L. Hay

*FOUR ACTS OF PERSONAL POWER: How to Heal Your Past
and Create a Positive Future,* by Denise Linn

*INNER PEACE FOR BUSY WOMEN: Balancing Work, Family,
and Your Inner Life,* by Joan Z. Borysenko, Ph.D.

*THE KEYS: Open the Door to True Empowerment and Infinite
Possibilities,* by Denise Marek and Sharon Quirt (available July 2009)

LEFT TO TELL: Discovering God Amidst the Rwandan Holocaust,
by Immaculée Ilibagiza, with Steve Erwin

REPOTTING: 10 Steps for Redesigning Your Life,
by Diana Holman and Ginger Pape

THE SECRET PLEASURES OF MENOPAUSE,
by Christiane Northrup, M.D.

*TAPPING THE POWER WITHIN: A Path to Self-Empowerment for Women:
20th-Anniversary Edition,* by Iyanla Vanzant

❧ ❧ ❧

All of the above are available at your local bookstore,
or may be ordered by contacting Hay House (see last page).

We hope you enjoyed this Hay House book. If you'd like to receive a free catalog featuring additional Hay House books and products, or if you'd like information about the Hay Foundation, please contact:

Hay House, Inc.
P.O. Box 5100
Carlsbad, CA 92018-5100

(760) 431-7695 or **(800) 654-5126**
(760) 431-6948 (fax) or **(800) 650-5115 (fax)**
www.hayhouse.com® • **www.hayfoundation.org**

Published and distributed in Australia by: Hay House Australia Pty. Ltd., 18/36 Ralph St., Alexandria NSW 2015 • *Phone:* 612-9669-4299 *Fax:* 612-9669-4144 • www.hayhouse.com.au

Published and distributed in the United Kingdom by: Hay House UK, Ltd., 292B Kensal Rd., London W10 5BE • *Phone:* 44-20-8962-1230 *Fax:* 44-20-8962-1239 • www.hayhouse.co.uk

Published and distributed in the Republic of South Africa by: Hay House SA (Pty), Ltd., P.O. Box 990, Witkoppen 2068 • *Phone/Fax:* 27-11-467-8904 orders@psdprom.co.za • www.hayhouse.co.za

Published in India by: Hay House Publishers India, Muskaan Complex, Plot No. 3, B-2, Vasant Kunj, New Delhi 110 070 • *Phone:* 91-11-4176-1620 *Fax:* 91-11-4176-1630 • www.hayhouse.co.in

Distributed in Canada by: Raincoast, 9050 Shaughnessy St., Vancouver, B.C. V6P 6E5 • *Phone:* (604) 323-7100 • *Fax:* (604) 323-2600 www.raincoast.com

Tune in to **HayHouseRadio.com®** for the best in inspirational talk radio featuring top Hay House authors! And, sign up via the Hay House USA Website to receive the Hay House online newsletter and stay informed about what's going on with your favorite authors. You'll receive bimonthly announcements about Discounts and Offers, Special Events, Product Highlights, Free Excerpts, Giveaways, and more!
www.hayhouse.com®